THE FRUGAL FOODIE
COOKBOOK

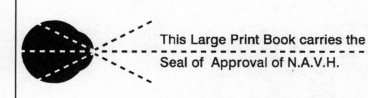

This Large Print Book carries the
Seal of Approval of N.A.V.H.

THE FRUGAL FOODIE COOKBOOK

{ WASTE-NOT RECIPES FOR THE WISE COOK }

BY LARA STARR
WITH LYNETTE SHIRK

THORNDIKE PRESS
A part of Gale, Cengage Learning

GALE
CENGAGE Learning

Detroit • New York • San Francisco • New Haven, Conn • Waterville, Maine • London

Copyright© 2009 by Lara Starr and Lynette Shirk.

Thorndike Press, a part of Gale, Cengage Learning.

LIBRARY OF CONGRESS CATALOGING-IN-PUBLICATION DATA

Starr, Lara Morris.
    The frugal foodie cookbook : waste-not recipes for the wise
cook / by Lara Starr with Lynette Shirk. — Large print ed.
      p. cm.
    ISBN-13: 978-1-4104-3123-3 (hardcover : Lg. print)
    ISBN-10: 1-4104-3123-1 (hardcover: Lg. print) 1. Low budget
cooking. 2. Large type books. I. Shirk, Lynette Rohrer. II. Title.
TX652.S664 2010
641.5'52—dc22

                                                        2010026911

Published in 2010 in arrangement with Cleis Press & Viva Editors.

*To my grandmother Naomi Spector
and my great-grandmother
Esna Fishman, who taught me
to be tight with my money
and open with my heart.*

— LARA STARR

TABLE OF CONTENTS

Storage and Safety

INTRODUCTION

I'm not a food snob, but I am a gourmet at heart. From humble street food to white-tablecloth dining to home cooking, I love good food. What I'm not hung up on is pretension. I'm equally content to savor an organic stone-fruit compote gateau as I am to gobble a peach cobbler. I appreciate a wedge of ripe triple-cream St. André as much as the next gourmet, but yes, I occasionally enjoy (gasp!) Cheez Whiz®. I grew up eating my great-grandmother's hand-stretched strudel and my mom's homemade éclairs along with Space Food Sticks and Tang, so let's just say my palate has range. This book is about keeping both our comfort-food-seeking souls and our sophisticated palates happy on a pauper's pocketbook. Assembled here are recipes, tricks, tips, and anecdotes from frugalistas past and present. Vintage wisdom combined with modern sophistication will help you strike a balance between the gourmet in your heart and the miser in your head.

Being frugal is about getting the most value from your food. It doesn't mean using absolutely the least expensive ingredients. You could probably pare your food budget down to pennies if you lived on potatoes and ramen noodles — but would you call that living? Making smart choices about how, when, and where you spend your money will fill your pantry and menus with delicious options. Splurge on a little balsamic vinegar and extra-virgin olive oil for salad dressings, and a few shallots and humble ingredients will come alive with flavor. Cooking at home is also a frugal alternative to going out. Of course you'll spend a lot less than if you'd gone to a restaurant, but cooking is its own pleasure and entertainment. After two hours in a movie theater, what have you got? Up to 100 fewer dollars in your pocket (movie tix, popcorn, parking, babysitter, it all adds up) and the pleasure of sitting next to a screaming baby or amorous teens. Spend that same two hours at home and teach yourself a new culinary trick, or try a new recipe. You'll have more money in your pocket and a delicious treat — it's win–win! Once you start getting into the frugal mind-set, it's hard to stop looking for ways to stretch your dollar and find value. I recently tossed a bunch of pine boughs (freshly collected after a wind-storm — I call it "Seattle roadkill") in the back of my hatchback to serve as car air freshener. It lasted longer than one of those rearview-mirror danglers, smelled way better, and it was *free!*

I've been fortunate to work in some of the best kitchens in the world, Chez Panisse, Masa's, and as a cook and recipe tester for Chuck Williams at Williams-Sonoma. With each experience, I saw examples of "foodie frugality" in action. Alice Waters elevated humble vegetables to haute heights by taking celery root, rhubarb, potatoes, and the like, and preparing them with attention and care. Suddenly, a yam could reveal flavors of great delicacy. Fennel, often considered a weed, could touch the palate with striking originality. She and many other great kitchen queens and kings now have their own veggie gardens, as well as a cadre of micro farms to supply them with the very best and freshest produce. You don't have to have a deep green thumb to grow a few of your own ingredients. It's surprisingly easy and soul-satisfying to assemble a dish using food you've grown yourself. A few hours of work and just a little bit of planning can save money, provide big flavor, and bring immense amounts of joy to your table. Start a micro garden in your front yard and you can grab the makings for a mixed green salad and dig up a few purple potatoes as you walk in the door from work.

Even if you replace just a few restaurant meals with homemade, make one loaf of bread or one batch of homemade oatmeal a week, or grow one or two veggies and herbs, you're a Frugal Foodie. You'll eat better, save money, and have more fun in the kitchen than ever. I hope you'll share your own tips and ideas, or photos and experiences of recipes you've made from this book. Let's create a Frugal Foodie community, and all feast from the table.

Bon appétit!
Lynette Shirk

CHAPTER 1
BANKABLE BREAKFASTS

Your mama was right. Breakfast is the most important meal of the day.

A healthy and hearty breakfast will make you more alert and productive (increasing your opportunities for raises and promotions, ka-ching!), fill you up so you'll be less likely to spend money on midday snacks, and if done right can be a yummy pleasure and calming morning meditation rather than a rushed chore.

MORNING FIX
When I was in college, I worked in an ice

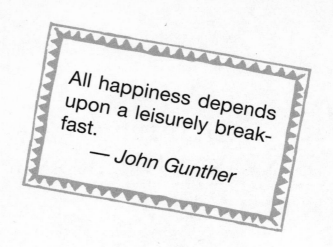

All happiness depends upon a leisurely break-fast.

— John Gunther

cream shop that also served espresso drinks — this was way before words like *barista* and *venti* had entered the vocabulary, and lattes and mochas were still somewhat exotic. I learned what a truly good cup of coffee tastes like, and became a lifelong and unrepentant java junkie. Getting a fix was cheap and easy as long as I was working at the shop, but very spendy when I was on my own.

I once caught a glimpse of the profit break-down for the various coffee drinks — the most expensive item had a 2,000 percent markup! Yikes! Great for the café's bottom line, but for the customer, not so much.

Most towns today have a gourmet coffee place on every corner — sometimes more than one — making it easy to develop an expensive daily coffee habit.

Giving up your lattes is the first thing

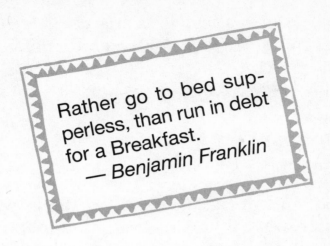

Rather go to bed supperless, than run in debt for a Breakfast.
— Benjamin Franklin

financial experts recommend when you're looking to economize, but you don't have to give up your morning fix or jolt of caffeine. Coffee drinks are easy to make and take less time than waiting in long lines at the shop or drive-through.

Roast Your Own Coffee

1/2 cup green coffee beans

Preheat oven to 450°F.

Spread coffee beans evenly in one layer in a cake pan. Roast for 15 minutes.

Remove from the oven and let cool completely.

Store cooled roasted beans in an airtight container for up to a week, or longer in the freezer.

Yields 1/2 cup roasted beans.

Steam Your Own Milk

1 cup milk

Heat milk in a saucepan on the stove or microwave it in a glass container until hot but not simmering or boiling. (Microwave time is about 20 seconds.)

Pour hot milk into a blender and hold the lid on tightly with a kitchen towel. Blend on high for 45 seconds.

Pour into a mug or to-go tumbler.

Coffee should be black as Hell, strong as death, and sweet as love.
— *Turkish Proverb*

FRUGAL FOODIE TIP: THE SKINNY ON MILK FAT

Did you know that nonfat milk makes better foam than low-fat or whole milk? It makes a latte with better body — and makes your body better too. Fat messes with the stability of the bubbles forming within the protein. It's the same reason that whipped egg whites need to be beaten with absolutely no yolk in them when making meringue.

Make Your Own Mocha

Mochas are even pricier than lattes at cafés, so kick the habit of spending without losing the luxury of sipping with this user-friendly recipe. You need to make the Hot Chocolate on a Spoon recipe from Chapter 9, Thrifty Gifts, and keep a few chocolate spoons stocked in the pantry. Technically, a mocha is made from espresso, but you can fudge it with coffee. There are economical espresso makers out there. I'm talking about those Italian stove-top versions. I often see them at thrift stores for less than five bucks.

1/2 cup hot espresso or coffee

1 Hot Chocolate on a Spoon (recipe, page 279)

3/4 cup steamed milk

Stir your Hot Chocolate on a Spoon into the steamed milk to make hot chocolate.

Pour the chocolate steamed milk into the espresso or coffee.

Makes 1 mocha.

FRUGAL FOODIE TIP: CHOCO-LATE ON THE CHEAP

If you don't have Hot Chocolate on a Spoon in stock, make a quick and cheap chocolate syrup by whisking a little bit of sweetened cocoa powder and just enough hot water to moisten it in the bottom of your cup before adding the coffee and milk.

Eggs are the wonder of the kitchen: inexpensive and nutritious, and they can be baked, boiled, fried, or scrambled into countless delectable dishes.

I'll never forget the day my son finally decided he liked to eat scrambled eggs. For years I had to pass up the good deals on 18-count or dozens that were buy one, get one free. Suddenly, a whole new world of savings and breakfast opportunities opened up. I could make up a big batch that would

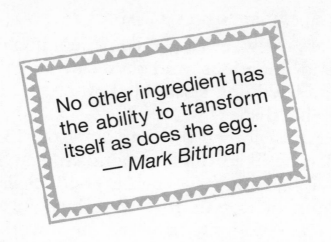

No other ingredient has the ability to transform itself as does the egg.
— Mark Bittman

feed the whole family, and he barely noticed when I snuck in a little meat or veggies as long as it was enrobed in a cloud of fluffy scrambled eggs.

Stretch Your Eggs Scramble

Wake up, stretch your legs, then stretch your eggs

I'll take advice from the fabulous Patti La-Belle on pretty much anything. In addition to being a disco diva and stage-stomping dynamo well into her sixties, she's authored several successful cookbooks that celebrate good health and great food. I once heard her say the secret to her scrambled eggs was a tiny bit of water, and of course, LaBelle is right. A teaspoon of water per egg is free, adds no fat or calories, and will give your scramble fluff and volume.

You can whip up a large batch of scrambled eggs on the weekend, and serve up hot and hearty breakfasts all week.

12 large eggs

1/4 cup water

salt and pepper

Preheat a 12-inch nonstick pan over medium-low heat.

Mix the eggs and water in a bowl with a fork until thoroughly blended.

Spray pan with nonstick cooking spray.

Add the egg mixture to the pan. Cook for 2–3 minutes, until the edges are cooked through. Thinking of your pan as a clock, start at 12:00 and scrape the edge of the eggs toward the middle with a wooden or nylon spoon. Tilt the pan to let the uncooked eggs spill over onto the pan surface. Continue scraping and tilting at 3:00, 6:00, and 9:00. Begin again at 12:00 and continue until the eggs have all been scraped to the middle of the pan. Fold the eggs over on themselves a couple of times until almost cooked through. If they look cooked in the pan, they'll be dry on the plate.

FRUGAL FOODIE TIP: COVER UP!

Keep scrambled eggs, pancakes, and other food piping hot with an inexpensive tortilla warmer.

Styrofoam warmers can be found for as little as a dollar at discount stores and Latino markets.

Put a saucer or plate in the bottom of the warmer, or line it with aluminum foil, and add your food to it as it comes out of the pan. Food stays hot while you finish the rest of your meal, and it won't dry out or use energy as it would in an oven. Qué bueno!

Season with salt and pepper, and serve.

Makes 6 servings.

See "Commuter Sammies" (page 28) for more ideas for leftover scrambled eggs.

Omelet Options

As with most simple dishes, the key to omelet success is technique. In *Kitchen Confidential* Anthony Bourdain famously recounts his "audition" for a chef's job: create a simple, perfect French omelet under the watchful eye of the restaurateur. Good cooks become great chefs when their passion and skill turn humble ingredients into delicious dishes.

Luckily you won't have monsieur looking over your shoulder while you do it, and you can master the foolproof method for creating a yummy, fluffy omelet.

3 large eggs

1/2 teaspoon water

salt and pepper, to taste

fillings of your choice

Mix the eggs, water, salt, and pepper in a bowl with a fork until blended, but don't overbeat.

Heat a 10-inch or 12-inch nonstick skillet over medium-low heat. Spray with non-stick cooking spray or coat with a bit of butter.

Add the egg mixture to the pan. As it cooks, stir it with a wooden or nylon spoon while shaking the pan over the heat. Scrape the cooked eggs from the sides of the pan and blend with the rest. The finished consistency should be like a chunky batter. This should take less than 1 minute.

When the eggs are just about set but still slightly wet, pat them into an even layer and let them cook undisturbed for a few seconds.

Add fillings, precooked if needed, down the center of the omelet.

Loosen around the edges of the omelet with the spoon. Tilt the pan to one side, scoot the spoon or a spatula under the opposite side of the omelet, and flip it to the middle to cover the fillings. Then tilt the pan to the other side and do the same with the other half of the omelet. Voilà!

Fill 'Er Up

Typical omelet fillings like bacon and sausage can get pricey and turn your cheap eggy breakfast into a luxury item. Here are a few ideas for tasty and inexpensive fillings.

SAUTÉED ZUCCHINI

Zukes abound in many gardens, either your own or your neighbors'. When you've had your fill of zucchini bread, try some in an omelet. Sauté 1/2 cup zucchini with 1/4 of an onion and fresh or dried tarragon.

FRUIT AND YOGURT

Omit the salt and pepper from the egg mixture and fill with sliced fresh fruit and tangy yogurt.

POTATOES, SOUR CREAM, AND CHIVES

Spread a good slather of sour cream down the center of the omelet, add thinly sliced cooked waxy potatoes, and sprinkle with chopped chives or green onions.

LAGSAMLET

Spread 3 tablespoons ricotta or cottage cheese, 3 tablespoons leftover spaghetti sauce, and a sprinkling of mozzarella.

OMLITO

Heat 3–4 tablespoons of refried beans, spread on omelet, and top with Cheddar cheese and jalapeño rings.

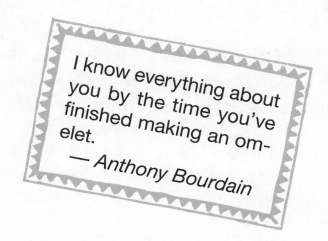

I know everything about you by the time you've finished making an omelet.

— Anthony Bourdain

BLINTZ-Y

Spread 2 tablespoons cream cheese and top with fresh or frozen blueberries OR blueberry jam.

HIPPY-DIPPY

Sprinkle with Jack cheese and top with alfalfa sprouts, diced tomatoes, and a slice or two of avocado.

Commuter Sammies

Oh, it's so easy to pull into the drive-through on your way to work or school and pick up a tasty portable sandwich to munch during your commute. Save a buck (or two, or three, or four) and make up a tasty sammie the night before while you're preparing dinner, and you can grab and go in the A.M.

Drive By — Not Through — the Golden Arches

Making your own egg, bacon, and cheese breakfast sandwich is tastier, healthier, and cheaper — what's not to love?

1 English muffin

2 teaspoons butter

2 thin slices mild Cheddar cheese

1 slice Canadian bacon

1 large egg

Top a toasted, buttered English muffin with thinly sliced Cheddar cheese.

Prepare the bacon and egg depending on how much time you have:

MORE TIME

Preheat a nonstick pan over medium-low heat. Lay an egg ring (or use a clean tuna can with top and bottom removed) in the pan and spray the pan and ring with nonstick cooking spray.

Crack the egg into the ring. Lay the bacon in the pan next to the ring.

Poke the yolk with a knife and let it flow into the whites. Cook for approximately 2 minutes, until the whites are firm.

Remove the ring from the egg. You may

need to run a knife around the outside of the egg to loosen it. Flip the egg over and cook for 1 minute.

Remove the egg from the pan and place it on the prepared English muffin.

Cook bacon approximately 1 minute more, until slightly browned. Remove from the pan and place it on top of the egg.

LESS TIME

Wrap the bacon in a paper towel and place it on a microwave-safe plate. Cook in the microwave for 1 minute.

Preheat a nonstick pan over medium-low heat. Beat an egg in a bowl with a fork to combine the white and yolk. Add the egg to the pan.

As the egg cooks, stir with a wooden or nylon spoon while shaking the pan over the heat. Scrape the cooked egg from the sides of the pan and blend with the rest. The finished consistency should be like a chunky batter. This should take less than 1 minute.

When the egg is just about set but still slightly wet, pat it into an even layer and let it sit undisturbed for a few seconds.

Remove the egg from the pan and place on

the prepared English muffin. Top with the cooked bacon.

NO TIME
Use leftover scrambled eggs or a slice of leftover savory omelet.

PB&J Pancakes

Spread leftover pancakes with peanut butter and jelly, add sliced bananas or strawberries, and sprinkle with granola.

Wafflewich

Spread leftover waffles with cream cheese and fill with bits of bacon.

Stuffed Muffins

Add 2 chopped cooked sausages and 4 chopped green onions to your favorite corn muffin batter. Fill muffin pans with batter, then top with shredded Cheddar cheese. Bake as directed, cool, and freeze. When you're ready for breakfast, pop a couple of muffins in a 350°F oven for 10–15 minutes. In the time it takes to brush and floss, you'll have a hot, toasty meal waiting for you.

Ándale Burrito

Fill a warm flour tortilla with scrambled

eggs, Cheddar cheese, refried beans, and sliced jalapeños. Roll up and wrap in plastic wrap. Store in the fridge for 3–5 days. Unwrap and microwave for 30–45 seconds, wrap in a napkin, and go!

FRUGAL FOODIE TIP: WHEN THING ARE DICEY — DICE!

To stretch pricey ingredients like meat, avocados, cheese, and nuts, dice or chop them and sprinkle on top of your dish, rather than mixing them in. You'll taste the yummy richness and flavor without having to use as much.

COZY OATS

One of the legends of frugal living, *Tightwad Gazette* founder Amy Dacyczyn, raised her family of eight on a single, modest military income. One of her strategies was a daily oatmeal breakfast. When I first read this I really felt bad for those kids, because I could only imagine a thin, sad Oliver Twistian bowl of porridge greeting them each day.

But if you put your mind to it, a humble bowl of oats can be tarted up in many tasty ways. A well-known national coffee chain has even gotten into the act, selling 10 cents' worth of oats for $3 a cup.

Make a big pot of oatmeal on Sunday, and you can serve it up all week, mixing it up with a variety of mix-ins and toppings.

Toasty Oatmeal

My great-grandma Mimi marveled when my mom made instant oatmeal for us kids. "Oy! We used to have to stand at the stove and stir, stir, stir," she said.

Going back to this old-fashioned technique will cost you a little bit of time, but there's a big payoff in the texture and flavor of your oatmeal.

This oatmeal uses water (free!) rather than milk, with a small amount of butter to add richness. Toasting the oats brings out the nutty flavor.

2 1/2 tablespoons unsalted butter

2 1/2 cups steel-cut oats (not instant or quick-cooking)

7–8 cups boiling water

1/2 teaspoon salt

In a large heavy-bottomed pot with a lid, melt the butter over medium heat. Add the oats and toast them, stirring often, until they smell nutty, about 3 to 4 minutes.

Stir in the boiling water and cover the pot. Stir frequently, about every 5 minutes.

After about 15 minutes, if the oatmeal is too thick, add water 1/4 cup at a time until it reaches the desired consistency. Continue cooking and stirring for another 10–15 minutes.

To make ahead, let the oatmeal cool completely and store in an airtight container in the fridge for up to 7 days.

Makes 7 servings.

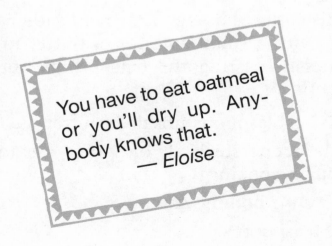

You have to eat oatmeal or you'll dry up. Anybody knows that.
— *Eloise*

Sow Your Own Oats

I've noticed instant oatmeal packets popping up in offices a lot, and it makes sense. A steaming bowl of oatmeal is like a warm hug for your tummy in the middle of a hectic workday. But you don't have to look for love in expensive, sugar-filled packets. It's easy to make your own instant oatmeal that can be popped in your purse or bag.

Homemade Instant Oatmeal Mix

2 1/2 cups instant oats

5 teaspoons light brown sugar

1 cup raisins or other dried fruit

3 tablespoons dry milk powder

Mix all of the ingredients in a bowl and portion into 5 servings in reusable containers.

To serve: Add 3/4 cup very hot water to 1 serving of the mix. Let stand until thickened, 3–4 minutes. Add more water a tablespoon at a time if the oatmeal is too thick.

Makes 5 servings.

Oatmeal Raisin Freezer Scones

That national coffee chain that shall remain nameless also ropes 'em in with an assortment of scones. You can save lots of money — and calories — by making nutritious scones yourself. Home-baked scones freeze like a dream and taste so much better than the ones you buy at the café. Pop one out of the freezer and into the oven while you pour your coffee, and in the time it takes to get dressed, a hot, fragrant treat will be waiting to ride with you to work.

2 cups flour

1 cup old-fashioned rolled oats

⅓ cup light brown sugar

2 1/2 teaspoons baking powder

1/2 teaspoon baking soda

1/2 teaspoon salt

1 1/2 sticks unsalted butter, chilled

3/4 cup raisins

1 cup + 1 tablespoon milk, divided

2 tablespoons granulated sugar

1/2 teaspoon ground cinnamon

Preheat oven to 400°F.

Put the flour, oats, brown sugar, baking powder, baking soda, and salt in the bowl of a food processor. Pulse 10–12 times. Cut the butter into 1 tablespoon pieces and distribute over the dry ingredients. Pulse until the mixture resembles coarse meal. Transfer to a bowl and mix in the raisins.

Add 1 cup milk and mix until blended. Gather into a ball with floured hands and divide in half. On a floured surface, pat half of the dough into an 8-inch round. Cut into 8 wedges. Repeat with the remaining dough.

Transfer the wedges to a lightly greased cookie sheet. Bake for 12–15 minutes,

FRUGAL FOODIE TIP: PROCESSOR POINTERS

To keep the blade from falling into your food when you dump the contents, stick your index finger into the hole on the bottom and hold it in place.

To soak your used processor bowl before washing it, place a clean, empty film canister, prescription bottle, or spice jar over the center stem — you'll be able to fill the bowl with soapy water all the way to the top.

until scones are firm to the touch and golden.

While the scones are baking, mix 1 tablespoon milk with the granulated sugar and the cinnamon. Remove the scones from the oven and brush them with the glaze while still hot.

Serve warm or at room temperature. To freeze, cool completely and store in a heavy-duty freezer bag, or wrap in plastic wrap and foil.

Makes 16 scones.

Oatmeal Smoothie

OK, stay with me on this one. When someone first suggested I try an oatmeal smoothie, I was kind of skeptical, but I was soon won over. The oatmeal adds body and a luscious texture to this meal-in-a-cup, as well as a boost of fiber.

If you've ever been shocked by the calories (and cost!) of the offerings at the popular megasmoothie outlets, you'll be soothed by these satisfying, smaller versions that rely on inexpensive ingredients and are a great way to use the bounty of summer berry vines.

Banana berry

1/2 cup old-fashioned rolled oats

1 cup pineapple juice

1 fresh or frozen banana, sliced

1/4 cup fresh or frozen berries

PB&J

1/2 cup old-fashioned rolled oats

1 cup milk

2 tablespoons peanut butter

1/4 cup fresh raspberries OR 2 tablespoons raspberry jam

1/2 cup ice

Apple crisp

1/2 cup old-fashioned rolled oats

1 cup apple juice

1/2 cup applesauce

1 teaspoon ground cinnamon

1 teaspoon brown sugar

1/2 cup ice

It's a Sunshine Day

1/2 cup old-fashioned rolled oats

1 cup pineapple juice

1 cup cantaloupe

1/2 cup ice

Orange Creamsicle®

1/2 cup old-fashioned rolled oats
1 cup orange juice
1 container or 1 cup vanilla yogurt
1/2 cup ice

Pick your smoothie ingredients and mix in a blender until smooth. Sweeten with sugar or honey, to taste.

Each recipe makes 1 large or 2 small servings.

3-IN-1 EYE-OPENER MIX
(AKA YOUR OWN PERSONAL BISQUICK)

Open your eyes to a world of breakfast possibilities — without opening a box — by creating your own all-purpose breakfast mix. The mix costs a fraction of the prefab versions from the supermarket, and it keeps well for months.

8 cups all-purpose flour

1/3 cup baking powder

1 tablespoon kosher salt

3 tablespoons sugar

8 ounces (2 sticks) unsalted butter

Mix the flour, baking powder, salt, and sugar in a large bowl with a wire whisk.

Cut the butter into small chunks and add them to the dry mixture. Toss the butter around to coat, and then use a pastry cutter or slash two knives across each other to cut the butter chunks into smaller pieces. Keep cutting until the mixture is sandy in consistency. You can also use a stand mixer with the paddle attachment for this step.

Store in freezer bags or an airtight container in the freezer for up to 3 months.

Makes 9 cups dry mix.

Biscuits

2 cups Eye-Opener Mix

1 cup milk or buttermilk

Preheat oven to 400°F.

Grease a muffin tin with vegetable oil spray.

In a large bowl, mix the milk and Eye-Opener Mix with a wooden spoon until combined. Then beat the dough briskly with the wooden spoon for 30 seconds.

Using 2 spoons, drop 1/4 cup dough into each muffin cup. Bake for 12 minutes.

Remove biscuits from the oven and serve warm, slathered with butter and drizzled with honey or molasses.

Makes 12 biscuits.

Pancakes

2 cups Eye-Opener Mix

1 1/2 cups milk

butter for cooking and garnishing

maple syrup

Preheat a griddle or large nonstick frying pan over medium to medium-high heat. (It's ready when butter foams on it. Turn the heat down to cook the 'cakes because you don't want the butter to burn.)

Mix the milk and the Eye-Opener Mix until the batter is blended, but don't overmix. It's OK if it's a little lumpy.

Butter the griddle, then scoop a scant 1/4 cup batter for each pancake onto it. When bubbles appear on the pancakes and start to pop, and the edges are set, flip the pancakes and cook another half minute or so.

Serve hot with butter and syrup.

Makes 16 4-inch pancakes.

FRUGAL FOODIE TIP: PAN-CAKES PAN OUT

If you have a large heavy-duty roasting pan with a flat bottom, you can put it over two burners on your stovetop to make a large griddle.

Waffles

4 eggs

2 tablespoons vegetable oil

2 cups milk

2 teaspoons vanilla extract

4 cups Eye-Opener Mix

Separate the eggs, putting the yolks in a bowl large enough to accommodate the final batter.

Whip the egg whites until they form soft peaks, and set aside.

Using a whisk, beat the egg yolks with the oil, milk, and vanilla extract. Whisk in the biscuit mix, and then lightly whisk half of the egg whites into the mixture.

Fold the remaining egg whites into the batter with a rubber spatula.

Preheat the waffle iron and spray with nonstick cooking spray right before adding the batter. Use 1 cup batter for each waffle, cooking for about 4 minutes, or until the waffle iron stops steaming.

Makes 6 7-inch round waffles.

CENTS-ABLE SOLUTIONS: COST-CUTTING CLEANUP CONCOCTIONS

A kitchen that's getting more use will need to be cleaned more often, and the more time you spend in there, the more grime you'll see. When I was young and single and the kitchen was just a place to store frozen diet dinners and tequila, I once dropped a fork and came face to face with the horror that was the floor behind my fridge. Shudder.

No one's going to pretend that cleaning the kitchen is fun or easy. The cheapest and most effective cleanser will always be elbow grease, but it can be easy on your wallet — and the environment — to use you own homemade cleansers.

- Baking soda is a great scouring paste for countertops and grout. Mix it with a little vinegar for a thrifty sink scrubber.
- Windows sparkle when you spray them with a mixture of 1 tablespoon

of white vinegar or ammonia per 1 cup water, then wipe dry with newspaper.

- Ammonia is a great nontoxic oven cleaner. Fill a bowl with 2–3 cups of ammonia and leave it in the oven overnight. Then wipe up food spills with warm water. The ammonia can still be used to clean floors and windows.
- For more stubborn oven stains, mix 1 cup salt, 1 cup baking soda, a squirt of dish soap, and enough white vinegar to make a paste. Spread it all over the inside of the oven and let it sit overnight. Wipe clean with warm water.
- Spray fruits and veggies with a mixture of 1 cup water, 1 tablespoon white vinegar, and 2 tablespoons baking soda, then rinse with water to remove dirt and chemicals.
- Mix up your own multipurpose cleaner in a clean gallon jug:

  3/4 cup baking soda
  3 tablespoons dish soap
  3/4 cup ammonia

6 tablespoons white vinegar
3 quarts warm water

Use directly on floors or in spray bottles for general cleaning.

- Stretch your dish soap by mixing it with equal parts water and storing it in a pump bottle.

I'm a marvelous housekeeper, every time I leave a man I keep his house.
— Zsa Zsa Gabor

I hate housework. You make the beds, you wash the dishes and six months later you have to start all over again.
— Joan Rivers

FRUGAL FOODIE TIP: SWITCH-A-ROO

My mom was a very young mother and got a lot of advice from the other moms in our co-op nursery school. One tip she passed on from them was to wipe down all the switch plates for lights and all the places you push on interior doors once a week. The house will feel much cleaner even if you haven't done a major attack.

FRUGAL FOODIE TIP: CLEAN UP WHEN YOU'RE DOWN

There's a lot of downtime in the kitchen. While your food is marinating, baking, cooling, or soaking, tackle one easy cleanup project, like wiping down a shelf in the fridge or giving the sink a scrub.

CENTS-ABLE SOLUTIONS:
MEAL PLANNING 101

You can avoid both overshopping and undershopping by setting aside a few minutes over the weekend to plan out your meals for the week. There are countless benefits to meal planning. You won't find yourself roaming the aisles desperate for inspiration for the evening's meal, and you won't be tempted by the expensive prepared foods in the in-store delis. And when you buy what you need for the week, you'll save time and money on midweek trips to the store.

Dinners

On the day you do your shopping, make a list of the dinners you'll have for the week, including the main dish and any veggies and sides. If you're making a "big dish" like pasta or a roast, you can slot in "leftover night" as well. Then, make a grocery list of all of the items you'll need to prepare the week's menu.

You'll know exactly what you need and don't.

Post the week's menu on the fridge, and save them up for a few weeks — you'll build a repertoire of your family's favorite dishes.

Lunches

Most kids are happy to eat the same thing over and over again, but neither man nor child can live on peanut butter and jelly alone. Foods like pizza, quesadillas, and even homemade chicken nuggets are perfectly palatable to kids at room temperature and make great lunches.

To keep yourself sane and your kids healthy and happy, make a five-day menu that can be repeated week to week. Monday could be pizza day, Tuesday bagel and cream cheese day, etc. Supplement the main dish with fruit or cut-up veggies and something crunchy, like crackers, dry cereal, pretzels, or rice cakes. These "sides" keep well and are easy to grab if junior wants to dip into his lunchbox at recess.

Breakfasts

Weekday breakfasts are usually quick affairs. Save your big cooking guns for the weekend, when you can make waffles, pancakes, and quiches that can last for several meals. It takes only minimally more time and trouble to make two quiches than to make one, and you'll have a hearty slice of eggy goodness ready for weekday breakfast.

> Life is too complicated not to be orderly.
> — Martha Stewart

> Organizing is what you do before you do something so that when you do it it is not all mixed up.
> — Winnie the Pooh

CHAPTER 2
BRUNCHES —
WHEN YOUR WALLET
DOESN'T HAVE BUNCHES!

A lazy weekend brunch is one of life's cheap thrills. A soul- and tummy-warming assortment of sweet and savory yummies, served with plenty of hot coffee and a thick, juicy newspaper. And you save money by combining two meals into one!

Brunch has a rich history in Chinese American and Jewish American cultures. Chinese families can be found crowding dim sum houses on Sunday mornings, choosing delectable dumplings from roving carts. And in brownstones and rest homes from Brooklyn to Florida, *bubbes* and *zaydies* consider

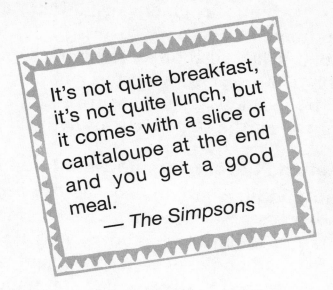

It's not quite breakfast, it's not quite lunch, but it comes with a slice of cantaloupe at the end and you get a good meal.

— *The Simpsons*

no Sunday complete without bagels, lox, and the *New York Times*.

Brunch is also an economical way to entertain at home. The food is simple, alcohol is not required, and it's a nice way for families to get together without disrupting kids' bedtimes.

CRAVEABLE CASSEROLES

While the term *casserole* may conjure images of condensed-soup gloop with indistinguishable vegetables, the culinary tradition of one-dish meals is rich and delicious. Consider French cassoulet, the king of casseroles. The humble combination of sausage, duck, beans, and vegetables is elevated to gourmet heights by slow cooking in a single pan and

53

is just at home in chichi restaurants as on Grandmère's table.

A big, baked dish of something warm and bubbly is a great way to start your brunch, and the delicious aromas wafting from your oven will set the stage for a lovely meal.

Sweet and Savory Tomato Bread Pudding

Bread puddings are an excellent way to use bread that's past its prime. The main ingredients are inexpensive staples, and the flavors can be endlessly varied depending on the veggies and herbs you have on hand.

5 cups sturdy bread cubes, such as sourdough, sweet baguette, or ciabatta

2 tablespoons butter

2 tablespoons brown sugar

1 clove garlic, chopped

2 pounds tomatoes, seeded and cut into chunks

2 tablespoons balsamic vinegar

2 tablespoons fresh herbs, any combination of basil, chives, parsley, tarragon, sage, thyme, or marjoram

1/2 teaspoon salt

freshly ground black pepper

4 large eggs

2 cups milk

Preheat oven to 350°F.

Toast the bread cubes on an ungreased baking sheet until golden brown, about 10 minutes. Let the bread cool while you make the custard.

Melt the butter in a heavy skillet over medium-low heat. Add the brown sugar, stir, and cook until smooth. Add the garlic and cook for 2–3 minutes. Add the tomatoes, vinegar, and herbs and cook until just heated through, about 3–5 minutes. Season with salt and pepper.

Whisk the eggs and milk in a large bowl. Add the bread cubes and tomato mixture. Allow to sit for 10 minutes so the bread can absorb some of the custard.

Turn the mixture into well-buttered 2-quart baking dish. Bake at 350°F until firm to the touch, 40–45 minutes. Serve warm.

To make ahead, assemble the pudding up to 2 hours before baking. Store in the fridge wrapped in plastic wrap. Bread cubes can be toasted up to 24 hours in advance and stored airtight at room temperature.

Serves 6–8.

Hands-Free Hash Browns

1 large white onion, diced

2 large garlic cloves, minced

4 tablespoons olive oil

3 pounds waxy potatoes (white, Yukon gold, red, or blue), very thinly sliced

1/2 cup (one stick) butter, melted

1 teaspoon salt

freshly ground pepper

Preheat oven to 350°F.

Butter a 3- to 4-quart baking dish.

Heat 1 tablespoon olive oil in a large skillet over medium-high heat. Add the onion and sauté for 3–4 minutes. Add the garlic and cook for 1–2 minutes more. Toss the potatoes with the remaining oil and the butter, onion, garlic, salt, and a few grinds of pepper. Transfer to the prepared dish and cover with foil. The dish can be made ahead to this point and stored in the fridge overnight.

Remove from the fridge and allow to return to room temperature. Bake for 20 minutes. Remove the foil, increase oven temperature to 450°F, and continue to bake until top is browned and crisp,

about 25 minutes more.
Serves 6–8.

Tout le Fruit Crisp

A warm, bubbly fruit crisp is ideal for brunch. It's a one-dish dessert that's not too sweet, and if you make it at the end of the week or on Sunday you can use up an assortment of fruit from the week that might not make it until Monday. Or, if you're lucky enough to have access to wild blackberries, this is a great way to use the luscious fruit you've braved the thorns to collect.

FILLING

6 cups assorted berries and fruit, such as peeled and sliced apples, pears, peaches, persimmons, or plums
2 tablespoons flour
3/4 cup sugar

TOPPING

1 cup flour
1/2 cup granulated sugar
1/2 cup brown sugar
1 teaspoon baking powder
1 egg, beaten
1 stick unsalted butter, melted

Preheat oven to 375°F.

Mix the fruit, flour, and 3/4 cup sugar in a large bowl. Let stand while you prepare the topping.

Blend the flour, the sugars, and the baking powder in a medium bowl. Add the egg and blend with the dry ingredients until crumbly.

Turn the fruit mixture into a well-buttered glass or ceramic baking dish. Evenly distribute the topping mixture over the fruit. Drizzle the melted butter evenly over the topping.

Place the baking dish on a cookie sheet or rimmed baking sheet to catch any over-flowing juices. Bake the crisp until the topping is set and golden brown, 45–55 minutes.

Serve warm or at room temperature.

To make ahead, the topping mixture can be assembled and stored in the fridge for up to 24 hours.

Serves 6.

NAKED QUICHES

Save time and money by leaving the crust off your quiche, and spend your effort and dollars on yummy fillings.

A thin coating of breadcrumbs helps the quiche release easily from the pie plate, and browns to an attractive golden color.

Green Goodness

2 tablespoons dry breadcrumbs (see page 64 for tip for making your own breadcrumbs)

1 (10-ounce) package frozen chopped spinach, kale, or collard greens, thawed and drained OR 1 pound fresh greens such as spinach, kale, chard, escarole, arugula, chicory, or collard greens

2 tablespoons olive oil

2 cloves garlic, minced

1 cup finely sliced green onions

4 eggs, beaten

1 cup milk

2 cups shredded Swiss cheese

1/4 teaspoon salt

1/8 teaspoon freshly ground black pepper

Preheat oven to 350°F.

Butter a 9-inch glass pie plate and coat with the dry breadcrumbs.

First, prepare the greens. If using frozen, thaw the greens completely. Place in a fine strainer and press with a wooden spoon to remove as much liquid as possible. If using fresh, soak the greens in cool water. Drain, and trim all tough stems and less-than-fresh leaves. Chop coarsely. Bring a large pot of salted water to a boil and blanch the greens for 1 minute. Drain in a fine strainer and press with a wooden spoon to remove as much liquid as possible.

Heat oil in a large skillet over medium heat. Add garlic and onion and cook for 3–4 minutes. Stir in greens and continue cooking for 5–7 minutes until any remaining liquid has evaporated.

In a large bowl, combine eggs and milk. Add cheese, greens, salt, and pepper, and stir to blend. Transfer to prepared pie plate.

Bake until eggs have set, about 30 minutes.

Let cool for 10 minutes before serving. *Serves 6.*

Swap Meat

Swap in your favorite meat in this rib-sticking quiche any "real man" will love to eat.

2 tablespoons dry breadcrumbs (see page 64 for tip for making your own breadcrumbs)

1/2 pound lean ground beef, ground pork, or sausage mix OR 1 cup diced ham OR 1/2 pound sausage links

1 small yellow onion, chopped

2 cloves garlic, minced

1/2 pound white or brown mushrooms, cleaned and sliced

4 eggs, beaten

1 cup milk

2 cups shredded sharp Cheddar cheese

1/4 teaspoon salt

1/8 teaspoon freshly ground black pepper

Preheat oven to 350°F.

Butter a 9-inch glass pie plate and coat with the dry breadcrumbs.

Preheat a 12-inch skillet over medium heat. Add your choice of meat and cook thoroughly. Remove the meat from the pan and set aside. Drain off most of the grease, leaving about 1 teaspoon in the pan. Add onion and cook until translucent, about 4–5 minutes. Add garlic and cook for 3–4 minutes. Add mushrooms and cook, stirring occasionally, for 8–10 minutes.

In a large bowl, combine eggs and milk. Add cheese, meat and mushroom mixture, salt, and pepper, and stir to blend. Transfer to prepared pie plate.

Bake until eggs have set, about 30 minutes. Let cool for 10 minutes before serving.

Serves 6.

Cheese, Please

We're going to add a little bit of luxury to this quiche in the form of a shallot. Shallots offer a unique flavor that's a little like onion, a little like garlic, and a lot like delicious. A handful of shallots is a relatively economical splurge, and one of the reasons restaurant food tastes so good is that professional chefs use them much more often than most home cooks.

Shredded cheese freezes beautifully. If you find yourself with an odd bit of cheese in the fridge, shred it and store it in a heavy-duty freezer bag. When you've saved up 3 cups of cheese you can make this yummy dish.

- 2 tablespoons dry breadcrumbs (see page 64 for tip for making your own breadcrumbs)
- 2 tablespoons unsalted butter
- 2 large shallots, minced
- 4 eggs, beaten
- 1 cup milk
- 3 cups shredded mild cheese — any combination of Monterey Jack, Colby, Edam, Swiss, Gouda, Fontina, or Muenster
- 2 tablespoons chopped fresh flat-leaf parsley
- 1/4 teaspoon salt
- 1/8 teaspoon freshly ground black pepper

Preheat oven to 350°F.

Butter a 9-inch glass pie plate and coat with the dry breadcrumbs.

Melt butter in a 12-inch skillet over medium-low heat. Add the shallots and sauté until translucent, about 4–5 minutes.

In a large bowl, combine eggs and milk. Add cheese, parsley, shallots, salt, and pepper and stir to combine. Transfer mixture to prepared pie plate.

Bake until eggs have set, about 30 minutes. Let cool for 10 minutes before serving.

Serves 6.

WAFFLE BITES

Make your brunch feel like a real party by serving waffles as bite-sized appetizers. Cut the waffles into 1-inch pieces and top with spreads and toppings.

4 waffles (recipe, page 44)

**FRUGAL FOODIE TIP:
DIY DRY BREADCRUMBS**

Let stale bread get good and hard. Place chunks in a food processor and pulse into crumbs. Or, if you just want a bit, grate the bread over the small holes of a hand grater, or place it in a ziplock bag and crush with a rolling pin or kitchen mallet. Store airtight in the fridge for up to 2 weeks or in the freezer for up to 2 months.

VARIATIONS

Cornmeal: Replace 1/2 cup of the Eye-Opener Mix with cornmeal

Oatmeal: Replace 1/2 cup of the Eye-Opener Mix with oatmeal

Buttermilk: Replace the whole milk with buttermilk

SPREADS AND TOPPINGS

Whipped cream and berries

Cream cheese and smoked salmon

Yogurt cheese (see tip below) and sliced fruit

Peanut butter and honey

FRUGAL FOODIE TIP: SAY YOGURT CHEESE

It's easy to turn yogurt into a cream cheese–like spread. Line a fine sieve with cheesecloth or coffee filters and fill with plain or fruit-flavored yogurt. Set the sieve over a bowl and chill for 24 hours.

CENTS-ABLE SOLUTIONS: BE A HIPPER CLIPPER

The Frugal Foodie doesn't use many coupons. Most of the coupons found online or in the Sunday paper are for expensive processed food that you wouldn't look at twice if you didn't have that little slip of paper in your pocket. And when you really stop and look at the coupons, the savings don't always add up. Thirty cents off two cans of soup? Whoop-dee-do. That isn't going to get you any closer to retirement. You're much better off with a store brand, or better yet, making your own.

That said, from time to time coupons cross your path that are worth the trouble. Here are a few tips for making the most of coupons, sales, and specials.

- Keep coupons in your wallet. Since you won't be using dozens of coupons, you can keep the good ones in your wallet without taking up too much space, and you'll never forget them at home.

- When you make your grocery list, take a peek at your coupon stash and list those items and the coupon value as well. That way, when you go to buy something like cream cheese, you'll see on your list that you have a 25-cent coupon, and can determine if it's a good deal or if another brand is cheaper.
- Bigger isn't always better. Many items are cheaper in large sizes, but some are not. (Don't ask me to explain it!) Make sure to check the shelf tag for the price per ounce or price per pound to make sure you're getting the best deal.
- The back of your grocery receipt is often printed with coupons that you might be interested in using. They are usually for local businesses and offer discounts for things like car washes and dry cleaning.
- Pay attention when checking out. This isn't the time to chat on the phone or clean out your purse. Even the most well-meaning

checker can miss a coupon or key in the wrong item. I once bought a half gallon of ice cream and a bunch of bananas and was charged almost $60! It turned out that a $50 gift card had made its way onto the belt and was charged to my bill. A $10 gift card could easily get "lost" in a grocery bill of $100 or more.

- Many sale items are priced in multiples, such as "10 for $10," but most stores don't require you to buy 10 of the items; you can buy only as many as you need for $1 each.
- Charm your checker. If you shop at the same store frequently, a little kindness can go a long way. Smile and say hello, glance at their name badge and get to know their name. A friendly checker will let you know if you're buying a buy one, get one free that you may not have noticed, or slip you an extra coupon.
- Eat before you shop. You'll end up with a lot fewer impulse items if your tummy isn't being tempted by

the food porn on the packaged items or the fresh bread smells wafting from the bakery.

- If at all possible, leave the rugrats at home. You'll have much more patience for choosing the freshest produce and comparing prices if Junior isn't clinging to your ankles and screaming for a cookie. I love taking advantage of open-till-midnight and 24-hour stores and shopping after the kids are in bed. You've practically got the whole place to yourself and can sashay right through the checkout line.
- Get in the habit of making a grocery list throughout the week. Keep a chalkboard or dry-erase board on the fridge, and as soon as you run out of eggs, sugar, dish soap, etc. write it on the board. It's very easy for these items to hide from you when it's time to write your list for the store. To give your memo board the look of a French bistro menu, remove the glass from a thrift-store picture frame and spray it with

chalkboard paint. Replace the glass and attach the frame to your fridge with super-strong magnets.

Eating is not merely a material pleasure. Eating well gives a spectacular joy to life and contributes immensely to goodwill and happy companionship. It is of great importance to the morale.

— *Elsa Schiaparelli*

CHAPTER 3
MIDDAY MONEY MATTERS:
LUNCH FOR LESS

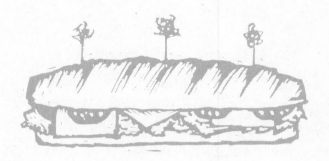

Lots of people spend their mornings looking forward to lunch — it's the first break in
the work or school day. And, since many of
us either skip breakfast or gobble something
quick and easy, it might be the first decent
meal of your day.

A weekend lunch can also be a great way
to entertain. The midday meal can be more
relaxed than dinner, and in nice weather it
can be enjoyed in the backyard, at a park, or
at the beach.

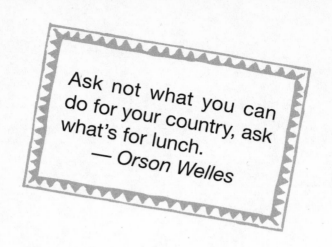

Ask not what you can
do for your country, ask
what's for lunch.
— Orson Welles

BROWN-BAGGIN' IT

When you're uninspired by what's in your
brown bag, it's all too easy to be tempted
by well-meaning co-workers to go out for
a pricey restaurant meal. I should know. I
used to bring soup to work, fully intending
to eat the sensible if boring lunch. Invariably
my co-workers would convince me to go out
for Chinese food, take-out deli sandwiches,
or, when I was really bad, to the chichi retro
diner with the $15 hamburgers.

My husband's co-worker was at the other
extreme. This well-paid attorney's daily
lunch consisted of a brick of ramen noodles
fortified by handfuls of saltine crackers
swiped from the deli in the lobby. He heated
up the ramen in the microwave and added
enough crackers to make a thick porridge.
Just looking at the bowl of goo would have

been enough to make most people queasy, but nothing made this guy happier than his 15-cent lunch.

With a little planning, you can reach a happy midday medium: a tasty and appealing lunch that won't break the bank.

All-American Asian Slaw

A solid salad that will stay crisp for several hours in a lunchbox. Almonds are a bit of an indulgence, but you can shave off a few dollars by buying whole raw almonds from the bulk bin and toasting them yourself. If you chop them fine and use sparingly, every bite of salad will have the rich flavor of tasty almonds.

Sesame oil is another splurge, but a little goes a long way and it adds a distinctive fla-

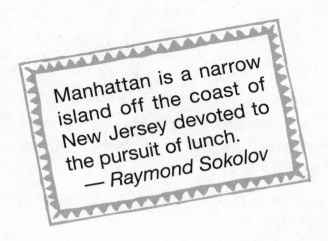

Manhattan is a narrow island off the coast of New Jersey devoted to the pursuit of lunch.
— Raymond Sokolov

vor to the dressing.

Whole bone-in chicken breasts are much less expensive than boneless and skinless, and have a much better flavor. By poaching the chicken you'll make a nice portion of chicken broth to use another time.

Even picky eaters will love the sweet dressing and crunchy toppings. To make it more fun, pack the noodles in a separate container and the kids can add them in at the lunch table.

You can prepare the salad entirely from scratch or, since time is money, speed it up with the help of a couple of convenience items from the grocery store.

SALAD

1/2 cup whole raw almonds

1 whole chicken breast, bone-in

3 cloves garlic, peeled

1/4 small white onion, thinly sliced

1/4 cup parsley

1 carrot, cut into 1-inch pieces

8 square won ton wrappers OR 1 cup chow mein noodles OR 1 package ramen noodles

1/2 cup vegetable oil (for preparing won ton strips)

1 15-ounce bag of coleslaw mix OR 1 large
head of green cabbage, shredded

2 green onions, sliced

DRESSING

1/2 cup vegetable oil

1 tablespoon sesame oil

1 tablespoon sugar

3 tablespoons seasoned rice vinegar

2 tablespoons soy sauce

TOAST THE ALMONDS

Preheat a heavy skillet over medium-high heat. Add the almonds to the pan and toast, stirring constantly, until the nuts are fragrant and golden, about 8–10 minutes. Remove the nuts to a cutting board and allow them to cool completely. Chop finely in a food processor.

PREPARE THE CHICKEN

Place the chicken, garlic, white onion, parsley, and carrot in a pot with a tight-fitting lid. Add 6 cups of water and bring to a simmer over medium-high heat. Cover the pot and simmer for 20 minutes. Remove the chicken from the broth and allow to cool. Strain the vegetables from the broth and discard. Reserve the broth for another use.

When the chicken has cooled, remove the meat from the bones and shred finely with your hands.

CRISP THE WON TON STRIPS

Preheat oven to 400°F.

Slice the won ton wrappers into 1/4-inch strips. Place strips on a rimmed baking sheet, and drizzle the oil evenly over them. Bake until crisp and golden, 5–7 minutes. Remove to a paper-lined plate (tip, page 81).

ASSEMBLE THE SALAD

Assemble the chicken, coleslaw mix or cabbage, and green onions in a large bowl. Whisk the dressing ingredients in a small bowl, add to the salad, and toss to coat completely. Add the almonds and toss again. Add the won ton strips or noodles just before serving.

Serves 4–6.

Three-Day Sandwich

You and your family will eat like kings from this majestic sandwich. The flavors continue to mix and mingle and improve with age for up to 3 days in the fridge.

The inside of the bread loaf is scooped out and can be used for making breadcrumbs (tip, page 64), bread pudding (recipe, page 54), or croutons (tip, page 82).

You can vary the vegetable and meat toppings to suit your taste. Zucchini alla Scapece (fried and marinated zucchini flavored with mint) is both traditional and a great use for abundant garden produce.

This sandwich makes prudent use of luxurious prosciutto, goat cheese, and balsamic vinegar. To make your dollars stretch even further, replace these ingredients with ham, cream cheese, and red wine vinegar. The sammie will be a little less authentic but just as delish.

- 1 loaf rustic Italian bread, such as ciabatta or Pugliese
- 1 large garlic clove
- 1 tablespoon balsamic vinegar
- 6 tablespoons olive oil
- 8 ounces goat cheese, room temperature
- 1/2 cup Tapenade (recipe follows)
- 2 cups Zucchini alla Scapece (recipe follows)
- 6 ounces prosciutto, thinly sliced
- 2 cups loosely packed basil, arugula, or spinach (any combination)

Slice loaf of bread horizontally. Remove the soft bread from both halves of the loaf, leaving about a 1/2-inch bread shell. Reserve scooped-out bread for another use.

Prepare the dressing. With the blade running, put the garlic clove down the feed tube of a food processor and mince fine. Add the balsamic vinegar and pulse 2–3 times. Slowly add 5 tablespoons of the olive oil. Set dressing aside.

Brush the bottom half of the bread with remaining 1 tablespoon olive oil. Spread the goat cheese over it and top with tapenade. Add the zucchini in an even layer. Drizzle half of the dressing over the sandwich. Layer on the prosciutto and drizzle with the remaining dressing. Scatter herbs/spinach over the sandwich. Place the top crust on the sandwich.

Wrap the sandwich tightly with plastic wrap or parchment paper. Place a rimmed baking sheet or cookie sheet on top of the wrapped sandwich. Place a heavy weight such as a brick or large cast-iron skillet on top of the baking sheet, and let it sit at room temperature for at least 1 hour.

Store the sandwich tightly wrapped in the fridge, and cut off slices as you need them for up to 3 days.

Makes 8–10 servings.

Zucchini alla Scapece

1 pound zucchini, thinly sliced crosswise

1/2 cup olive oil

3 garlic cloves, peeled and minced

1 tablespoon mint leaves, chopped

3 tablespoons red wine vinegar

salt

Heat olive oil in a frying pan over medium heat. Test the oil with a piece of zucchini. If it sizzles when added to the oil, the oil is ready for frying.

Add zucchini slices one at a time in a single layer. Fry for 3–5 minutes on each side, until golden brown. Remove zucchini to a paper-lined plate (tip, page 81) and repeat with remaining zucchini slices. Reserve leftover olive oil.

In a large bowl, combine fried zucchini slices, garlic, and mint. Drizzle with 2 tablespoons of the reserved olive oil and the vinegar and mix gently. Season with salt, to taste.

Cover the bowl with plastic wrap and let the mixture sit at room temperature for 1–2 hours.

Makes 2 cups.

Tapenade

1/2 pound kalamata olives, pitted

3 tablespoons capers, drained

4 anchovy fillets

1 garlic clove

1/2 cup olive oil

1 tablespoon lemon juice

salt and pepper, to taste

Combine the olives, capers, anchovies, and garlic in a food processor fitted with a steel blade, and pulse 3 times. Add the olive oil and lemon juice, and process until chunky. Season with salt and pepper.

Makes about 2 cups.

FRUGAL FOODIE TIP: FRY PAPER

Instead of using a pile of paper towels for draining fried foods, put a layer of newspaper, a paper grocery bag, or a dish towel on the plate, then use just a single paper towel as the top layer that touches the food.

FRUGAL FOODIE TIP: CAPER CRUSADER

The smaller end of a melon baller is great for getting capers out of a jar; the hole in the scoop drains the brine as you pull it out.

Deconstructed — and Reconstructed — Antipasto

Antipasto means "before the meal" and is traditionally a beautifully arranged first-course platter of meats, cheeses, and veggies that signifies the start of an Italian meal. We're going to deconstruct that artful arrangement, and then reconstruct it into several meals.

MASTER ANTIPASTO

10 cups vegetables, at least three of the following:

broccoli, florets and stalks, cut into 1-inch pieces

zucchini, cut into 1/2-inch pieces

cauliflower, florets and stalks, cut into 1-inch pieces

mushrooms, brushed clean and quartered

tomatoes, seeded and cut into 1-inch pieces, or halved cherry tomatoes

green or red peppers, seeded and cut into 1-inch pieces

carrots, scrubbed and cut into 1/2-inch pieces

red onion, peeled, quartered, cut into 1-inch pieces

DRESSING

1 cup olive oil

1/4 cup red wine vinegar

1/4 cup balsamic vinegar

1 1/2 tablespoons sugar

4 garlic cloves, minced

salt and pepper

One day in advance, put all of the dressing ingredients into a jar with a tight-fitting lid and shake well to combine. Leave at room temperature, shaking every so often.

Assemble the vegetables in a large lidded container. Pour the dressing over the veggies and stir to combine. Chill in the fridge for at least 6 hours before serving.

Makes 10 servings.

Antipasto Lunches

GREEN SALAD

Top crisp greens with 1 cup of veggies for a hearty, healthy salad.

SANDWICH

Fill a pita pocket with veggies and add a slice of cheese.

FRITTATA

Beat 3 eggs with 2 tablespoons milk. Add 1/2 cup chopped veggies. Pour into a ramekin, top with shredded cheese, and bake for 20 minutes in a 350°F oven.

SOUP

Coarsely chop 1 cup of veggies and add to chicken broth or tomato soup.

PIZZA

Top prebaked or homemade pizza crust (recipe, page 151) with a thin layer of shredded mozzarella, a layer of marinated veggies, and another thin layer of cheese. Bake at 450°F until browned and bubbly, approximately 10 minutes.

BENTO BOX

The lunch special at a local sushi restaurant is always tempting, and even more so when the alternative is a soggy sandwich in the bottom of your bag. Make your own Asian-inspired bento box and you'll be much less likely to give in.

Make lunch even more special by packing it in pretty containers that can be found in Asian markets and Chinatown shops for just a few dollars. Include a set of reusable chopsticks.

Asian cuisine is inherently frugal, relying on lots of vegetables and using expensive proteins sparingly.

Sushi Salad

6 cups cooked white rice

1 large cucumber, peeled, seeded, and diced

1/2 pound cooked crabmeat, picked over

1 large ripe avocado, peeled and diced

DRESSING

1/2 cup seasoned rice vinegar

1 tablespoon sesame oil

1 tablespoon sugar

1 1/2 teaspoons wasabi paste or prepared horseradish

Combine the dressing ingredients in a small bowl and whisk to blend. Pour the dressing over the rice and stir to coat completely. Add the cucumber, crab, and avocado and stir gently.

Makes 6 servings.

Peek-a-Boo Shrimp Rolls

A mere 1/2 pound of shrimp is stretched into 12 tasty rolls. The pretty, pink shrimp is visible through the thin rice-paper wrappers, giving you the sensation that you're eating lots of luxurious shrimp, but the roll is really filled out with inexpensive noodles and veggies.

1/2 pound uncooked, unpeeled shrimp

1 6-ounce package rice noodles, broken into 6-inch lengths

1/2 tablespoon sesame oil

12 8-inch-diameter round rice-paper wrappers

1 cup bean sprouts

1 large carrot, julienned or shredded

1 head romaine lettuce, shredded

1/4 cup thinly sliced basil (tip, page 89) or

chopped cilantro

DIPPING SAUCE

1/2 cup Asian fish sauce

1 tablespoon seasoned rice vinegar

1 large garlic clove, minced

1/4 cup sugar

2 tablespoons lime juice

1/2 teaspoon red pepper flakes

Bring 6 quarts of water to a boil. Add the shrimp and boil until bright pink, approximately 3 minutes. With a slotted spoon, remove the shrimp to a cutting board. Allow to cool, then peel and cut into 1/4-inch slices.

Add the rice noodles to the boiling water and cook until soft, approximately 3 minutes.

Place a large bowl in the sink with a sieve set over it. Drain the noodles in the sieve, reserving the hot water in the bowl. Rinse the noodles with cold water and place in a large bowl. Toss the noodles with the sesame oil.

To assemble the rolls, soak a rice-paper wrapper in the reserved hot water until soft, approximately 30 seconds. Lay the softened wrapper on a cutting board. Put slices of shrimp in a single row lengthwise down the center of the wrapper, leaving about 1 1/2 inches at the top and bottom. Layer the noodles, bean sprouts, carrot, and lettuce on top of the shrimp. Sprinkle with the basil or cilantro.

Fold the top and bottom of the wrapper over the filling. Then, starting at one side, roll tightly.

To make the dipping sauce, mix all ingredients in a bowl or lidded jar. Sauce can be made up to three days ahead and stored airtight in the fridge.

Makes 12 rolls.

Variation: Roll your own!

These rolls also make a fun, interactive appetizer. Omit the shredded romaine lettuce

and rice-paper wrappers. On a platter, make piles of each ingredient alongside whole leaves of butter lettuce and a small bowl of the dipping sauce. Let guests fill a leaf of lettuce with the noodles, shrimp, and veggies, then drizzle with the sauce, roll up like a burrito, and eat — delish!

FRUGAL FOODIE TIP: HERB HELPER

A *chiffonade,* or long, thin strips of leafy herbs such as basil, makes a pretty presentation when sprinkled on your dishes, and it makes just a handful of herbs go a long way.

Stack 5–6 leaves, then roll lengthwise. Your herbs will look like a little cigar. Starting at one end, slice the roll into thin ribbons.

Teriyaki Chicken "Skewers"

This stove-top version of teriyaki chicken is easy and delicious, and uses inexpensive chicken thighs. The chicken can be served over rice, or pack a serving into a container and eat it bite by bite with a toothpick.

3 pounds chicken thighs, bone-in

1 cup soy sauce

2 teaspoons sesame oil

3/4 cup white wine

3/4 cup chicken broth

2 tablespoons sugar

2 tablespoons honey

1/4 cup orange juice

1 large garlic clove, minced

Skin and debone the chicken thighs. Freeze the skin and bones for making broth at another time.

Mix the soy sauce, sesame oil, wine, broth, sugar, honey, orange juice, and garlic in a heavy lidded stockpot or large lidded skillet. Heat over medium heat until sugar is dissolved and sauce is smooth. Add the chicken thighs. Cover and simmer until chicken is just cooked through, around 30–40 minutes.

Remove the chicken to a cutting board, allow to cool slightly, and cut into 1 1/2-inch chunks.

Increase the heat and boil the sauce until reduced to 1 1/2 cups, about 15 minutes. Return the chicken chunks to the sauce and toss to combine.

Makes 6 servings.

DOWN-HOME AMERICAN DINER

Recreate classic lunch-counter favorites at home. You may miss the sassy waitresses, but not the hit to your pocketbook.

BLT Revisited

Rather than piling your sammie with lots of pricey bacon, make a delicious homemade mayonnaise studded with tasty bacon bits. Juicy tomatoes are the star of the sandwich.

1 strip good-quality thick-cut bacon

2 tablespoons mayonnaise (recipe follows, or use store-bought)

2 slices sturdy white or sourdough bread, toasted

1 medium-size ripe tomato, sliced

2 whole leaves romaine lettuce

Cook the bacon in a skillet until crisp, or

wrap in a paper towel, place on a microwave-safe plate, and microwave until crisp, approximately 1 1/2 minutes.

Crumble the bacon and mix with the mayonnaise. Chill for 1–2 hours to allow the flavors to develop. Spread the bread with the bacon-mayonnaise mixture. Pile on the sliced tomatoes and lettuce.

Serves 1.

Olive Oil Mayonnaise

1 whole egg + 1 egg yolk, room temperature

1 tablespoon lemon juice

1 tablespoon white wine vinegar

1/4 teaspoon sugar

1 teaspoon Dijon mustard

salt, to taste

1 cup olive oil

Put eggs, lemon juice, vinegar, sugar, mustard, and salt in the bowl of a food processor and pulse to blend. With the motor running, add the olive oil in a slow, steady stream until the mayonnaise is thick, stopping and scraping the bowl as needed.

Makes 1 cup.

Sweet-and-Sour Glazed Meatloaf

This diner standby makes delicious sandwiches, and is also yummy crumbled into an omelet or frittata.

This meatloaf is stretched with the addition of cooked rice and eggs, and fortified with lots of chopped veggies. As an alternative to the traditional ketchup topping, a quick and easy sweet-and-sour glaze is whipped up with pantry staples.

2 tablespoons olive oil

1 cup finely chopped celery

1 cup finely chopped onion

1 cup finely chopped green pepper

1 cup finely chopped carrot

1 garlic clove, minced

2 pounds lean ground beef

3 eggs

2 cups cooked white rice

1 teaspoon salt

1/2 teaspoon pepper

SWEET-AND-SOUR SAUCE

1 cup fresh tomato puree (recipe follows) or canned tomato sauce

1/4 cup brown sugar

1/4 cup red wine vinegar

1 1/2 tablespoons Dijon mustard

Preheat oven to 400°F.

Heat the oil in a large sauté pan over medium heat. Add the celery, onion, green pepper, carrot, and garlic, and cook, stirring, for 5 minutes, until the onion is translucent. Remove the vegetables to a large bowl.

Add the ground beef, eggs, rice, salt, and pepper to the veggies and mix with your hands until well blended. Pat the mixture into a large loaf pan. Cover the pan with foil and bake for 40 minutes.

While the meatloaf is baking, make the sweet-and-sour sauce. Combine the tomato puree (or tomato sauce), brown sugar, vinegar, and mustard in a saucepan and simmer until the sugar is dissolved. Keep warm.

Remove the meatloaf from the oven after 40 minutes, and turn the temperature down to 350°F. Remove any liquid fat from the meatloaf with a turkey baster, or blot with paper towels. Cover the meatloaf completely with warm glaze. Bake uncovered at 350°F for 20 minutes.

To serve immediately, allow to the meatloaf to rest for 10 minutes and then cut into slices. For sandwiches, allow the meatloaf to cool completely, remove from the pan, and wrap in foil. Slice as needed.

FRESH TOMATO PUREE

1 cup chopped fresh tomatoes

2 tablespoons red wine

salt and pepper, to taste

Simmer tomatoes and wine in a small saucepan for 15 minutes. Force the mixture through a sieve and season with salt and pepper.

Top It Off

Here are a few ideas for adding extra zip to your meatloaf sandwich.

SHARP CHEDDAR, ARUGULA LEAVES, AND THINLY SLICED RED ONION

BALSAMIC ONIONS

Slice an onion and sauté in 1 tablespoon

each butter and olive oil over low heat, until browned and caramelized. Add 2 teaspoons balsamic vinegar and stir to combine. Season with salt and pepper.

SLICED PICKLES AND FRESH TOMATOES

SUN-DRIED TOMATO SPREAD

Simmer 1 cup sun-dried tomatoes in red wine for 10 minutes, drain (reserving wine for later use in dressings or stews), and put in the bowl of a food processor. Add 1/2 cup olive oil, 2 peeled cloves of garlic, and 2 teaspoons red wine vinegar or balsamic vinegar. Process until smooth.

ROASTED PEPPERS

Coat seeded and quartered red or green peppers with vegetable oil. With the oven set to Broil, position a rack 2 inches from the flame and roast the peppers for 15–18 minutes, turning occasionally. The skins should be black and blistered. Put the peppers in a paper bag and seal the top. When the peppers have cooled, slide the skins off with your fingers.

Mock Potato Salad

Remember "mock apple pie"? Same concept, with saltine crackers instead of Ritz.

2 sleeves saltine crackers (about 80 crackers)

1/2 cup diced onion

1/2 cup diced celery

1/2 cup pickle relish

1/2 cup chopped green onions

3 hard-boiled eggs, peeled and chopped

2 cups mayonnaise (maybe more)

1/4 cup Dijon mustard

Tabasco sauce, to taste

Crush the saltine crackers in a large bowl.

Add the remaining ingredients and stir to combine. Add more mayo if needed until the ingredients are well coated and hold together. Chill for an hour before serving. You may need to add more mayo again before serving if the salad appears dry.

Makes 6 servings.

LADIES LUNCHIN'

A weekend lunch is a lovely way to entertain your gal pals. Because the meal is lighter and no wine or alcohol need be served, it's a less expensive option than a dinner or cocktail party.

THE HISTORY OF THE BLUE PLATE SPECIAL

"Blue plate specials" were common on American diner menus beginning in the 1920s. The entire meal was served on a single divided plate, rather than in individual dishes, as you'd see at fancier joints. The most common manufacturer of divided plates made them only in blue. The specials consisted of a meat and three vegetables for as little as two bits (25 cents).

The phrase "No substitutions" was a common fixture of the blue plate special menu, as immortalized in a line from the 1959 movie *Our Man in Havana:* "I can't bear French fries, but there's no pick and choose with a blue plate. You eat what you're given. That's democracy, man."

A Hawaiian variation is called the "plate lunch": two scoops of rice, a scoop of macaroni salad, and a serving of Japanese-inspired meat such as panko-crusted chicken or teriyaki beef. The plate lunch evolved when locals, immigrants, and servicemen worked together during WWII and shared their food at lunch.

DINER LINGO DECODED

Diner lingo is a system of saucy short-hand commands and nicknames developed by servers and cooks in the late 1880s. Though it is now hardly ever heard in the food service business, many terms, such as *eighty-six* and *B.L.T.,* have entered the common lexicon.

Adam and Eve on a raft: poached eggs on toast

burn the Brits: toasted English muffin

cow feed: salad

drag it through the garden: sandwich with all the veggies on it

eighty-six: to remove an item from an order or from the menu

first lady: spareribs (refers to Eve being made from Adam's rib)

gravel train: sugar bowl

heart attack on a rack: biscuits and gravy

in the weeds: an overwhelmed cook or waiter

joe: coffee

keep off the grass: no lettuce

let it walk: take-away order

moo juice: milk
Noah's boy: ham (Ham was one of Noah's sons)
on a rail: fast
pin a rose: with onions
quail: Hungarian goulash
sea dust: salt
two cows, make 'em cry: two hamburgers with onions
Vermont: maple syrup
whistleberries: beans
zeppelin: sausage

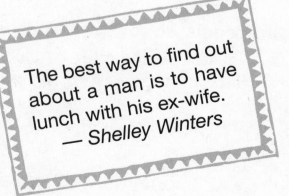

The best way to find out about a man is to have lunch with his ex-wife.
— *Shelley Winters*

> Don't think of Diana Vreeland's memoir as a book; it's more like a lunch. A bit of soufflé, a glass of Champagne, some green grapes — light, bubbly and slightly tart — all served up by an egocentric but inventive hostess.
> — Cathleen McGuigan, reviewing the memoir of the legendary Vogue editor

Versatile Veggie Soup

This is a master recipe that can accommodate a variety of veggies depending on the season, from asparagus in the spring to potatoes in the winter.

2 tablespoons butter

1 large white onion, peeled and chopped

2 tablespoons flour

6 cups chicken or vegetable broth

2 pounds vegetables (see guide below)

1 tablespoon fresh or 1 teaspoon dried herbs and spices (see guide)

salt and pepper, to taste

optional toppings and add-ins (see guide)

Heat the butter in a large stockpot. Add the onion and cook until translucent, about 5 minutes. Sprinkle the flour over the onion and cook for 2–3 minutes.

Add the broth, veggies, and herbs to the pot. Turn heat to high and bring the broth to a boil. Cover and simmer for 20–25 minutes, until veggies are fork tender.

Puree the soup with a hand blender until smooth, or in 1 1/2-cup batches in a regular blender. Season with salt and pepper. Serve warm or chilled.

Serves 4–6.

VEGGIE	HERB OR SPICE	TOPPING OR ADD-IN
zucchini	thyme	dollop of sour cream
carrots	ground ginger	swirl of plain yogurt
asparagus	tarragon	squeeze of fresh lemon juice
broccoli	ground nutmeg	grated sharp Cheddar
russet potatoes	rosemary	thinly sliced green onions
sweet potatoes	ground cinnamon	chopped toasted pecans
tomatoes	basil	shredded Parmesan cheese

FRUGAL FOODIE TIP: SOUP SHIELD

Use the lid of the pot to scrape veggies from the cutting board into the soup pot. It will act as a shield and keep hot liquid from splashing back on you.

It is impossible to think of any good meal, no matter how plain or el-egant, without soup or bread in it.
— *M.F.K. Fisher*

Best-Dressed Salad

Here's a frugal formula for a perfect green salad:

greens + savory + sweet + crunchy + master dressing = yummy

By limiting the number of ingredients in your salad, you'll shop for less produce, which means less produce that has an opportunity to spoil. You'll also have more distinct flavors than "kitchen sink" salads.

8 cups (about 4 large handfuls) greens, torn into bite-sized pieces

1/2 cup savory item (guide, page 108)

1/2 cup sweet item (guide, page 108)

1 cup crunchy item (guide, page 108)

MASTER DRESSING

4 tablespoons oil

1 tablespoon vinegar

1/4 teaspoon Dijon mustard

1/4 teaspoon salt

pinch of sugar

dress-up (optional add-ins — guide, page 108)

Toss the greens with the savory and sweet items in a large bowl.

Whisk the dressing ingredients (including optional dress-up) in a bowl, or shake in a lidded jar. Just before serving, toss salad with dressing to coat evenly, and sprinkle with crunchy item.

Serves 4.

Use the guide on the next page and have fun creating your own best-dressed salads.

FRUGAL FOODIE TIP: FREE SALAD SPINNER

Plastic salad spinners are expensive and take up a lot of valuable counter space. A clean cotton pillowcase makes a great salad spinner. Wash the greens and place them in the bottom of the case. Gather the top closed, step outside, and swing your arm like a windmill. The centrifugal force will pull the water from the leaves.

GREENS	SAVORY	SWEET	CRUNCHY	OIL	VINEGAR	DRESS-UP
red leaf lettuce	slivered red onion	chopped red apple	toasted almonds	extra virgin olive	white wine	1 tbsp minced shallot
romaine lettuce	crumbled bacon	tomatoes	croutons	extra virgin olive	balsamic	1 tbsp mayonnaise
spinach	sliced scallions	golden raisins	toasted pine nuts	extra virgin olive	red wine	1 clove minced garlic
butter lettuce	blue cheese	pear	toasted pecans	extra virgin olive	cider	squeeze of fresh lemon juice
iceberg lettuce	bean sprouts	shredded carrot	fried won tons or noodles	3 tbsp canola + 1 tbsp sesame	seasoned rice	1/4 tsp grated fresh ginger

FRUGAL FOODIE TIP: WRAP IT UP!

Don't toss leftover salad! While dressed salad won't last long in the fridge, it's delicious the next day wrapped in a warm pita or tortilla.

> To make a good salad is to be a brilliant diplomatist — the problem is entirely the same in both cases. To know exactly how much oil one must put with one's vinegar.
> — Oscar Wilde

No-Knead Dough

I love the double meaning of this easy–to–make bread. There's no kneading, so the bread is easy to make even for a beginning baker, and you don't need a lot of dough to make this yummy accompaniment to soup and salad. And as a bonus, your house will smell delicious when the bread is baking.

Mark Bittman kicked off the no-knead bread sensation in 2006 when he first published the recipe and method in the *New York Times*. There are scores of adaptations and variations on the recipe. This one is a little quicker, but just as tasty.

3 cups all-purpose flour

3/4 teaspoon active dry yeast

1/2 teaspoon sugar

1 1/2 teaspoons salt

1 1/2 cups warm water

1/2 teaspoon vinegar (balsamic, wine, or cider — whatever you have)

Mix all of the ingredients in a large bowl. The dough will be thick and gloppy. Cover the bowl with plastic wrap and drape with a kitchen towel. Leave it in a warm spot in your kitchen. The oven works well; just make sure you put a note on it reminding you that it's in there! Let the dough rise for about 6 hours. A little more or less is fine.

Spray a cutting board with cooking oil spray (or film with a little olive oil) and turn the dough onto the board. Shape the dough into a round loaf and cover it with the plastic wrap and towel. Let it rest for about an hour.

Thirty minutes before the dough is ready, preheat the oven to 450°F.

Put a Dutch oven, lidded casserole (ceramic, not glass), or other heavy lidded pot into the oven to preheat.

Scrape or pour the dough into the heated pot. The dough will be very wet — don't fret.

Bake for 30–35 minutes. Remove the lid and bake for 15–20 minutes more, until the top is browned and crusty.

Serves 4–6 as a side to salad or soup.

Sparkle Plenty Punch

Serve a refreshing punch in place of wine or cocktails at your ladies' lunch.

1 2-liter bottle club soda

2 cups iced herbal tea (see guide below)

2 cups fruit juice (see guide)

1/4 cup Simple Seed Syrup (recipe page 286)

TO MAKE AHEAD

The night before, mix all ingredients in a large bowl. Funnel the punch into two 2-liter plastic bottles and store in the fridge. Serve in ice-filled glasses.

TO SERVE THE SAME DAY

Assemble all of the ingredients in a large bowl. Ladle into ice-filled glasses.

or

Set out all of the ingredients bar style and let the ladies mix their own mocktails. *Makes 12 servings.*

TEA	JUICE
ginger	orange
mint	grapefruit
cinnamon	apple
berry	pomegranate
chamomile	pear nectar

Corny Napkin Holders

Craft these adorable napkin holders for a beautifully dressed table!

4 empty toilet paper cardboard rolls

craft glue

1 cup of flat 1/4-inch to 1/2-inch buttons — either various shades of yellow for sweet corn or multicolored assortment for dried Indian corn

4 cloth napkins — green for sweet corn or goldenrod for dried Indian corn

Coat the toilet paper rolls with glue and affix buttons in rows to simulate ears of corn. Let dry.

Fold napkins like rocket-shaped paper airplanes.

Insert napkins into the corn holders and set the table.

Makes 4.

Noncooks think it's silly to invest two hours' work in two minutes' enjoyment; but if cooking is evanescent, so is the ballet.
— *Julia Child*

CENTS-ABLE SOLUTIONS: FOOD STORAGE AND SAFETY

Being frugal isn't about being miserly or buying the least expensive products or ingredients, but about getting the best value out of everything you purchase. We've all heard the advice to shop like Europeans, particularly Italians and Parisians, who shop daily and keep very little in their tiny kitchens. This is a lovely idea if you're lucky enough to live in the City of Light and are blessed with abundant street markets and cursed with tiny kitchens. Here in the U.S. of A., most of us have exactly the opposite: large kitchens and huge crowded markets we'd rather not visit more than once a week.

- Take an extra minute or two to properly store your groceries and leftovers, and you'll be eating well longer.
- Separate your fruits and veggies and store then in separate crisper draw-

ers. They each give off different gases and spoil on different schedules.

- Buying meat on sale and freezing it is a great way to save money, but be sure you protect your purchase from freezer burn! Double up the butcher's packaging by placing the meat in a ziplock bag or wrapping it in foil.
- If your pantry is prone to pests, protect dry kitchen products like flour, cornmeal, and other grains by storing in the fridge or freezer.
- Nothing's more disappointing than getting yourself all excited to make chocolate chip cookies only to find that your brown sugar has turned into a petrified rock! You can keep it soft and ready for baking with a cheap terra-cotta saucer. Buy a 3-inch terra-cotta saucer from a garden supply or hardware store. Soak it in water for 30 minutes. Snuggle it into your brown sugar and your sugar will stay soft and cookie-ready for 6 months per soak.

- Store potatoes and onions in a cool, dark place.
- Shredded cheese, such as Cheddar, Swiss, or mozzarella, freezes beautifully. Buy plenty when it goes on sale, shred it yourself, and save it in the freezer in ziplock bags. To get out as much air as possible, put a drinking straw down the side of the bag almost to the bottom, zip to the edge of the straw, suck out the air (the bag forms to the cheese just like those late-night infomercials for vacuum sealers — its cool!), then quickly remove the straw and seal up the bag.
- Keep dried herbs and spices away from the stove. The heat and steam from cooking will cause them to lose their flavor.
- Many items you're keeping in the fridge, such as squash, tomatoes, and oranges, will keep better on the counter at room temperature.
- Thaw frozen meat in the refrigerator, in the microwave, or under cold running water. Thawing on the

117

counter increases the risk of bacteria.

- Keep your refrigerator clean and
not overstuffed. Plenty of room for
air to circulate will keep food fresher
longer.
- Bread, bagels, pitas, and tortillas
keep very well in the freezer. Thaw
them as you need them on the
counter or in a low oven.
- Although it's tempting to store leftovers in their cooking pans, these
containers are not airtight and the
food will spoil faster. Muster up the
energy to transfer your lovingly prepared delectables to airtight containers or ziplock bags.

Chapter 4
Snacks on a Shoestring

When hunger strikes between meals, you're very vulnerable to the temptation to buy pricey snacks. Muffins at the coffee shop, chips in the vending machine, and candy in the racks at the check-out line are never more appealing then when you're really hungry.

Have a little something stashed away in your purse, in your car, or at the back of the fridge and you'll be only an arm's length away from satisfaction.

Flashback Candy
My first experiment with candy making was

Tell me what you eat, and I will tell you what you are.

— Anthelme Brillat-Savarin

less than illustrious. A friend and I were home alone after school and somehow figured out that we had the few ingredients needed to make caramel corn (sugar, water, and popcorn). Without adequate adult supervision, the result was a disaster. My pal and I sat in the corner of the kitchen clinging to each other in horror as billows of black clouds rose from the burned syrup in the saucepan.

Since then, I've discovered that making candy is surprisingly easy, and a lost art that deserves to be found.

These old-fashioned sweets are inspired by the depression-era moms who used inexpensive pantry staples and a little kitchen alchemy to create delicious treats.

Cracker Toffee

When you're craving a treat and have "nothing" in the cupboard, you probably have the ingredients to make this sweet 'n' salty treat.

1 sleeve saltine crackers (about 40 crackers)

2 sticks unsalted butter

1 cup packed brown sugar

Preheat oven to 350°F.

Arrange the crackers in an even layer on a well-greased rimmed cookie sheet. The edges of the crackers should all be touching, with go gaps between them.

Melt the butter and brown sugar in a small saucepan over medium-low heat, stirring constantly. Bring the mixture to a full boil, boil for 2 minutes, continuing to stir constantly. Pour the boiling syrup evenly over the crackers. Spread with a butter knife or spatula if needed.

Bake for 5 minutes, until the toffee is bubbly.

Remove the candy from the oven and cool completely. Break the toffee into bite-sized bits.

Makes 4 cups.

Toffee Twists

CHOCOLATE-TOPPED TOFFEE

When the toffee comes out of the oven, sprinkle 2 cups of chocolate chips over the top. Allow to sit for 1–2 minutes to melt the chocolate, then spread into an even layer with a spatula or butter knife.

NUTS ABOUT TOFFEE

Sprinkle 3/4 cup chopped toasted almonds, peanuts, or pecans over the bubbling toffee.

TOFFEE GRAHAMS

Replace the saltines with Graham crackers.

COFFEE TOFFEE

Add 1 tablespoon instant coffee to the sugar and butter.

SUGAR AND SPICY TOFFEE

Add 1 teaspoon ground cinnamon to the sugar and butter.

MATZO MUNCH

Replace the saltines with matzo and the butter with margarine for a treat that's kosher for Passover.

Kitty Litter Candy

This delicious chocolaty candy doesn't need expensive chocolate, because it uses cocoa powder. When you make it you'll see why it is so named.

2 cups sugar

2 tablespoons cocoa powder

1/2 cup milk

6 tablespoons butter

1/2 cup peanut butter

2 cups old-fashioned rolled oats

1/2 teaspoon vanilla extract

Combine the sugar and cocoa powder in a saucepan.

Stir in the milk and butter and bring the mixture to a boil. Cook for 2 minutes and remove from heat.

Stir in the peanut butter, oats, and vanilla.

Lay out waxed paper. Drop teaspoons of the mixture onto it and let it cool.

Makes 3 dozen candies.

Marshmallow Madness

My friend Daphne and I have an annual tradition of making homemade gifts for the holidays. Sometimes we sew, sometimes we bake, and one year we made homemade marshmallows. It was a super-fun way to spend the day. We mixed multiple batches in the morning, left for a movie while they firmed up, and came back to finish the job.

Homemade marshmallows have a lighter taste and texture than the commercial kind — and you can have fun experimenting with flavors and colors.

3 1/4-ounce envelopes unflavored gelatin

1 cup cold water

2 cups sugar

2/3 cup light corn syrup

1/4 teaspoon salt

2 teaspoons vanilla extract

2 tablespoons cornstarch

1 cup powdered sugar + more for dusting

Sprinkle gelatin over 1/2 cup cold water in the bowl of an electric mixer and let it sit for 10 minutes.

In a small saucepan, combine the sugar, corn syrup, and 1/2 cup water. Cook on medium-high heat until the mixture comes to a rapid boil. Boil until the mixture reaches 250°F on a candy thermometer.

Pour the boiling syrup into the gelatin and mix with the whisk attachment. Start slowly, and gradually increase the speed to medium-high and add the salt. The mixture will smell kind of funky and look like a goopy mess, but be patient — it will transform into a fluffy cloud of sweetness. Beat for 10–12 minutes, then stir in vanilla.

Spray a flexible spatula with vegetable oil spray, and scrape the marshmallow into a greased cookie sheet. Spread the top evenly.

Allow the mixture to sit for about 4 hours to set. Turn the candy out onto a cutting board sprinkled with powdered sugar. Cut into pieces with a sharp knife or pizza cutter.

Mix the cornstarch and powdered sugar in a shallow bowl. Drop marshmallows a few at a time into the bowl and toss to coat.

Makes about 40 marshmallows.

Variations

CREAMSICLE®

Add 1 teaspoon orange extract and a couple of drops of orange food coloring.

MOCHA

Dissolve 1 tablespoon instant coffee in 1 teaspoon of boiling water. Add it to the mix with the second 1/2 cup water.

COCOA

Replace 1/4 cup of the powdered sugar with unsweetened cocoa powder.

PEPPERMINT

Add 1 teaspoon mint extract and a couple of drops of red food coloring.

DIPPED

Dip the bottoms of the marshmallows in melted dark or white chocolate and set them on sheets of wax paper to dry.

DIRT-CHEAP SELF-FILLING CUPCAKES

Chocolate Cupcakes

- 3 cups flour
- 2 cups sugar
- 1/2 cup cocoa powder
- 2 teaspoons baking soda
- 1 teaspoon salt
- 2 cups cold water
- 2/3 cup vegetable oil
- 2 tablespoons white vinegar
- 2 teaspoons vanilla extract
- 1 recipe Cream Cheese Filling (recipe follows)
- 12 fluted paper muffin cups

Preheat oven to 325°F.

Insert muffin cups in a muffin tin and set aside.

Combine the flour, sugar, cocoa powder, baking soda, and salt in a mixing bowl.

Combine the water, oil, vinegar, and vanilla in a pitcher. Pour the wet ingredients into the dry ingredients and whip with an electric mixer on medium for 3 minutes.

Pour the batter into the prepared muffin cups. Top each cupcake with 1–2 tablespoons of the cream cheese filling.

Bake for 28 minutes. Cool before serving.

Makes 12 cupcakes.

Gingerbread Cupcakes

1/2 cup sugar

1/2 cup vegetable oil

1/2 cup molasses

1/2 cup boiling water

1 teaspoon baking soda

1 1/2 teaspoons ground ginger

1/4 teaspoon ground cinnamon

1 1/4 cups flour

1 egg, beaten

1 recipe Cream Cheese Filling (recipe follows)

9 fluted paper muffin cups

Preheat oven to 350°F.

Insert muffin cups in a muffin tin and set aside.

In a bowl, mix the sugar, oil, molasses, and boiling water.

In another bowl, mix the baking soda, ginger, cinnamon, and flour.

Whisk the wet ingredients into the dry ingredients, then mix in the egg.

Pour the batter into the prepared muffin tins. Top each cupcake with 1–2 tablespoons of the cream cheese filling.

Bake for 45 minutes. Cool before serving.

Makes 9 cupcakes.

Pumpkin Cupcakes

1/3 cup vegetable oil

1/4 cup milk

1 egg, beaten

2/3 cup pumpkin puree (homemade [cooked] or canned)

1 cup sugar

3/4 teaspoon baking soda

1/2 teaspoon salt

1/4 teaspoon ground ginger

1/4 teaspoon ground cinnamon

1/4 teaspoon ground nutmeg

1 cup flour

1 recipe Cream Cheese Filling (recipe follows)

12 fluted paper muffin cups

Preheat oven to 350°F.

Insert muffin cups in a muffin tin and set aside.

In a bowl, mix the oil, milk, egg, and pumpkin puree. In another bowl, mix the sugar, baking soda, salt, ginger, cinnamon, nutmeg, and flour.

Stir the dry ingredients into the wet ingredients, then scoop the batter into the prepared muffin tins. Top each cupcake with 1–2 tablespoons of the cream cheese filling. Bake for 25–30 minutes. Cool before serving.

Makes 12 cupcakes.

Cream Cheese Filling

8 ounces softened cream cheese

⅓ cup sugar

1 egg

pinch of salt

1 cup chocolate chips

Cream the cream cheese with an electric mixer until smooth.

Add sugar, egg, and salt and mix thoroughly.

Stir in the chocolate chips with a spatula.

A WAY WITH WINGS

Master Wing Recipe

While sometimes you crave sweet snacks, other times you may need something a little heartier. A shot of protein is a great boost when you're active, and the wings keep well in the fridge for up to a week.

Chicken wings are perfect little 3-or-4-bite snacks, and they are some of the cheapest meat you can buy.

3 pounds chicken wings

2 tablespoons olive oil

sauce of your choice (recipes follow)

Preheat oven to 350°F.

Line a rimmed baking sheet with foil. Brush foil with olive oil. With a sharp knife, cutting at the joint, separate the drummettes — the largest section (it looks like a miniature drumstick) — from the wingettes — the middle section. Chop off the wing tips — the 2-inch pointy section attached to the wingette — and reserve to use later for making broth or soup. Arrange the chicken drummettes and wingettes on the pan in an even layer.

Bake for 30 minutes. Drain off liquid and grease. Add the chicken to the sauce and coat evenly. Let the wings marinate in the sauce for 30 minutes.

Bake the wings for an additional 30 minutes, or until crispy.

Serves 6.

Sweet-and-Sour Orange Sauce

1/2 cup fresh orange juice

zest from one orange

1/2 cup white wine vinegar

⅓ cup granulated sugar

1 tablespoon chopped fresh rosemary

1/4 teaspoon salt

1 tablespoon vegetable oil

Combine all ingredients in a saucepan and place over medium heat. Simmer for 7–10 minutes, stirring occasionally.

Hot Tomato Sauce

1 6-ounce can tomato paste

1/4 cup water

2 tablespoons red wine vinegar

1 teaspoon Dijon mustard

1/4 cup brown sugar

1/4 teaspoon ground cinnamon

1/4 teaspoon salt

1 teaspoon red pepper flakes

1 tablespoon unsalted butter

Combine first 8 ingredients in a saucepan and place over medium heat. Simmer for 5–7 minutes, stirring occasionally. Remove from heat and add butter, stirring until it is melted.

Italiasian Savory Sauce

1 1/2 tablespoons olive oil

1/2 teaspoon salt

1/2 teaspoon pepper

1/2 cup balsamic vinegar

3 tablespoons soy sauce

1 teaspoon brown sugar

1 tablespoon unsalted butter

Combine first 6 ingredients in a saucepan over medium heat. Simmer for 10–12 minutes, stirring occasionally. Remove from heat and add butter, stirring until it is melted.

THE INVENTION OF THE BUFFALO WING

The most famous savory wing snack is the Buffalo Wing, named for its home-town, Buffalo, New York. The spicy wings were invented by Teressa and Frank Bellissimo, owners of the Anchor Bar. Late one night, their son and his pals arrived home from college, hungry. Most of the day's food was already put away, but Mrs. B had a pile of chicken wings intended for soup stock, a fryer full of hot oil, and some hot sauce. She dumped the wings in the oil, fried them up, anointed them with hot sauce, and served them to the hungry lads with leftover celery sticks and blue cheese dressing.

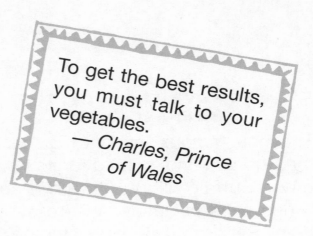

To get the best results, you must talk to your vegetables.
— Charles, Prince of Wales

CENTS-ABLE SOLUTIONS:
GROW YOUR OWN

While I love the idea of a bounty of fresh fruits, vegetables, and herbs right outside my door, I have a notoriously black thumb and a personal aversion to dirt. However, there are a few ways to add garden produce to your life with little time and effort. Garden as much as you have time, space, and energy for. Even a few garden items swapped in for supermarket produce will save you money, and it's

136

healthier for the body and soul. If you have more space than time, consider opening your yard to an apartment-dwelling friend or neighbor and let them work your land in exchange for some of the fruits (and veggies, and herbs) of their labor.

- One potato, two potato, three potato — more! Fill a barrel, tub, or stack of old tires with straw. Cut six or eight potatoes in half and nestle them into the middle of the straw with the eyes facing up. Water every week or so, and in about 3 months you'll have lots of new potatoes.
- Hang 'em high! Upside-down tomato growers are all the rage, but you can easily make your own. Cut a small hole in the bottom of a reusable polypropylene grocery bag with handles. Slip the vines of a small tomato plant through the hole and pack a damp strip of cloth around the hole on the inside of the bag. Fill the bag with soil and hang from a tree or plant hook. Water

from the open top of the bag every couple of days.

- Tomatoes can be grown in 5-gallon buckets placed on porches or balconies. Just drill a few holes in the bottom for drainage or fill the bottom with a couple of inches of gravel. Choose a "bush" variety that doesn't require stakes, to make it even easier. The built-in handles make them easy to move!
- Ginger grows very well indoors. Slice off a "finger" of ginger about 2 inches long. Fill a container half full of soil, add the ginger, and then fill the container to the top with soil. Keep the soil moist and you'll have lots of ginger within a couple of weeks.
- Make a block garden on a brick or cement patio. Cut open the long sides of a heavy-duty plastic lawn bag and spread it out flat. Cut drainage holes in the bag. Line the perimeter of the bag with concrete blocks and fill with soil. You can plant seeds, plants, and flowers.

Stick to "bushy" plants that don't require stakes.

- Save eggshells, coffee grounds, and vegetable peels and ends for compost. Layer the kitchen scraps with garden waste, newspaper, and soil in a large, lidded trash container, and throw in a handful of worms. Turn the compost every month or so.
- Sprout seeds in egg cartons, yogurt containers, or gallon jugs cut in half. Once a seedling has one or two true leaves, transplant it to a larger container.
- Make a minigreenhouse for sprouting seeds from a half-gallon milk jug cut in half or the clear plastic top from a bakery cake container.
- Discourage pests like gophers and squirrels naturally by planting garlic and onions with your flowers and veggies. Hang clangy wind chimes to keep the birds away.
- Newspaper is a natural weed killer. Cover the weeds with 4–5 layers of newspaper, then cover the paper

with soil, mulch, or clippings. After a few months the newspaper will break down and the weeds will be dead.

- To make a natural slug trap, sink a plastic container into the soil, leaving 1–2 inches above the ground. Fill the container with a couple of inches of beer.
- One part milk (not nonfat) to nine parts water makes a natural anti-fungal plant spray.

Chapter 5
Dinners on a Dime

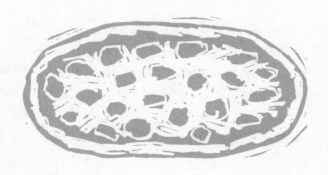

From family meals to romantic dining à deux, a tasty dinner feeds the body and the soul. The easiest way to overspend on dinner is to put off planning what to eat until late in the day. The siren call of the drive-through or pricey supermarket prepared meals can be downright deafening when you're hungry and short on time.

See page 49 for menu planning tips, and try these easy-to-make dishes that will please the whole family.

The Three P's: Pizza, Pasta, and Potatoes

Carby goodness, in the form of pizza, pasta, or potatoes, is the ideal frugal foundation for a hearty dinner. Fad diets aside, most of the world's traditional cultures base their healthy diets on starches.

Pasta Project

Have fun experimenting with different shapes of pastas and varieties of sauces. The key to success is boiling your pasta in plenty of salted water. (Italian grandmas say the water should "taste like the sea.") Don't add additional oil to the cooking water — it's a waste. Oil keeps the sauce from clinging well to the pasta.

Pasta should be cooked *al dente* — with a little bit of resistance to the tooth. Fish a noo-

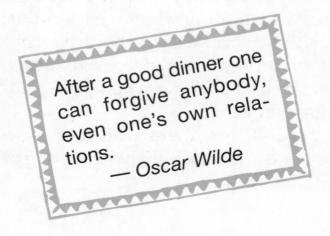

After a good dinner one can forgive anybody, even one's own relations.
— Oscar Wilde

dle out of the pot and give it a taste a minute before the recommended cooking time.

Tomato and basil sauce

4 tablespoons olive oil

2 pounds Roma tomatoes

2 cloves garlic, crushed

1/2 cup red wine

1/4 cup fresh basil, thinly sliced, or 1 1/2 tablespoons dried + a bit for garnish

salt and pepper, to taste

Preheat oven to 450°F.

Line a baking pan with foil. Add the whole tomatoes and drizzle with 2 table-spoons of the olive oil. Roast for 20–25 minutes, until the skins have started to blacken and split. Remove tomatoes from the oven and turn them over. Reduce the temperature to 350°F and continue roasting for 1 hour longer. Remove from the oven and let cool. Slip off the skins and roughly chop the tomatoes.

In a lidded skillet or saucepan over medium-low heat, gently sauté garlic in remaining 2 tablespoons olive oil, until softened. Add the roasted tomatoes, wine, and basil and stir to combine. Increase heat to medium-high and bring to a boil. Reduce heat, cover, and simmer for 30 minutes. Season with salt and pepper.

To serve, toss the sauce with warm pasta and sprinkle with additional basil.

Serves 4–6.

Peanut and peppers sauce

1 tablespoon canola oil

1 teaspoon sesame oil

4 cloves garlic, peeled and minced

4 teaspoons peeled, minced fresh ginger

1 red bell pepper, cored, seeded, and julienned

2 tablespoons soy sauce

1 1/2 tablespoons seasoned rice vinegar

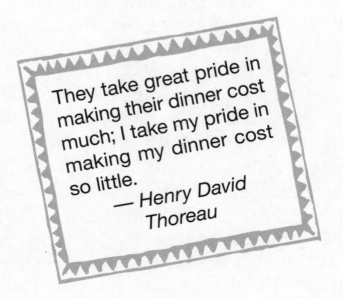

They take great pride in making their dinner cost much; I take my pride in making my dinner cost so little.
— *Henry David Thoreau*

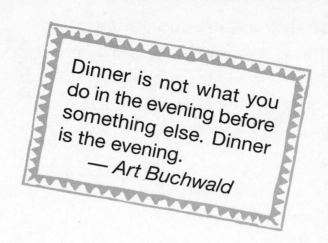

Dinner is not what you do in the evening before something else. Dinner is the evening.
— *Art Buchwald*

1 tablespoon brown sugar

1 teaspoon red pepper flakes

1 cup all-natural chunky peanut butter

1 cup vegetable broth

4 scallions, thinly sliced

Heat oils in a large skillet over low heat. Add garlic, ginger, and red bell pepper and sauté for 2–3 minutes. Add soy sauce, vinegar, sugar, red pepper flakes, peanut butter, and broth. Increase heat to medium and cook, stirring, until peanut butter melts. Simmer the sauce for 8–10 minutes.

Pour the sauce over cooked pasta and garnish with sliced scallions.

Lemon and asparagus sauce

1 pound asparagus, woody ends removed (tip, page 149), sliced into 1-inch lengths

3/4 cup vegetable broth

6 tablespoons butter

5 tablespoons olive oil

6 garlic cloves, minced

grated zest of 1 lemon

1/2 cup fresh lemon juice

1/2 lemon, very thinly sliced

1/4 cup chopped parsley (optional)

Preheat a covered skillet over medium-high heat. Add the asparagus, then pour the broth over the asparagus. Cover the skillet and steam for 5 minutes, until crisp-tender, and drain, reserving remaining broth. Return the broth to the pan and boil until reduced to 1 tablespoon.

Add the butter and olive oil to the reduced broth and cook until the butter is melted. Add garlic and sauté for 2–3 minutes. Add lemon zest, lemon juice, and sliced lemon and cook for 2–3 minutes. Add asparagus and toss to coat.

Pour the sauce over warm pasta, toss, and allow the pasta to absorb the sauce for a few minutes. Sprinkle with chopped parsley, and serve.

Greens and garlic sauce

6 cups vegetable broth

6 garlic cloves, thinly sliced

2 tablespoons olive oil

1 pound fresh spinach

salt and pepper, to taste

Boil the vegetable broth until reduced by about one-third in volume, approximately 15 minutes. Reduce heat and simmer the broth. Meanwhile, sauté the garlic in the olive oil until soft, about 5 minutes. Add the garlic with the oil and the spinach to the broth, and simmer just a few minutes, until the spinach is cooked through.

Pour the sauce over warm pasta and allow the pasta to absorb the sauce for a few minutes.

Squash and sage sauce

1 large butternut squash, peeled, seeded, and chopped into 1/2-inch cubes

8 tablespoons butter

40 fresh sage leaves, stemmed

2/3 cup vegetable broth

1/4 teaspoon ground cinnamon

salt and pepper, to taste

freshly grated Parmesan cheese (optional)

Melt 2 tablespoons butter over medium-low heat in a large stockpot. Add the squash cubes and sauté until tender, about 8–10 minutes. Remove the squash from the pot with a slotted spoon and set aside.

Melt the remaining 6 tablespoons butter in the pot. Add the sage leaves and cook until the edges start to curl, watching closely that the butter doesn't burn. Remove the sage leaves and set them on a paper towel to drain.

Add the broth and cinnamon to the butter and stir to combine. Add the pasta and toss to coat. Season with salt and pepper. Serve with the sage leaves and Parmesan.

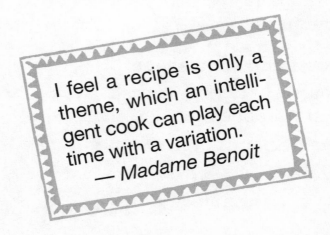

I feel a recipe is only a theme, which an intelligent cook can play each time with a variation.
— Madame Benoit

FRUGAL FOODIE TIP:
STALKING MADE EASY

To break off the woody end of a stalk of asparagus, hold the stalk with two hands. Grasping about 1 inch of the bottom end firmly with one hand, gently bend back the stalk with your other hand. The tough, woody bottom of the asparagus will naturally "snap" off, leaving a fresh, tender stalk.

NUTS? TRY DOUGH!

I was at a chain Mexican restaurant once with a bunch of stressed-out adults and antsy kids. The dead zone between ordering and the food arriving was threatening to turn into ground zero for toddler meltdown. Suddenly, like a white knight, the waiter appeared with a lump of tortilla dough for each of the kids. They were instantly entertained by pushing and pulling the dough and patting their own "tortillas." I thought it was a brilliant move by the restaurant. For the price of a lump of dough — just a few pennies — they bought my repeat business and a peaceful meal for the poor saps who had the misfortune of sitting next to us.

PIZZA PASSION

Make your own pizza and you've got both a fun family activity and a tasty meal. Kids love to help knead the dough and press it into the pan. Give them a little piece of their own dough to make a minipizza or breadstick.

Classic Pizza Dough

3 cups flour

2 teaspoons salt

1 1/2 teaspoons active dry yeast

1 cup lukewarm water

2 tablespoons olive oil + additional for oiling bowl and pan

cornmeal, for sprinkling

Stir flour, salt, and yeast with a wooden spoon in a large bowl. Add water and olive oil, and stir the mixture until you've got it as mixed as you can — there will still be some floury clumps. Turn the mixture onto a lightly floured surface. Knead the dough until it is a smooth ball.

Lightly oil the mixing bowl and return the dough to the bowl. Turn it over so all sides are coated with oil, and cover the bowl with plastic wrap. Lay a dish towel over the plastic wrap and leave the dough in a warm, dark place until doubled in size, about 2 hours.

Turn the dough back onto the floured surface and press it gently to remove the air. (At this stage, you can keep going and bake the dough, or store it in the fridge wrapped in plastic wrap for up to a week.)

Preheat oven to 450°F.

Lay the plastic wrap and towel back over the dough and let it rest for 15 minutes. Remove the wrap and knead the dough a couple more times. Roll or stretch the pizza to a 14-inch round. (Actually, mine always turns out more like a rounded rectangle.)

Oil a baking sheet and sprinkle with cornmeal. Transfer the dough to the baking sheet.

Prebake the crust on the lower rack of the oven for about 5 minutes. Remove from the oven and add the toppings (recipes follow). Return the pizza to the oven and bake until the crust is brown and crisp on the edges, the toppings are cooked through, and the cheese is melted — approximately 7–10 minutes, depending on the toppings. Let the pizza sit for 5 minutes before slicing.

Pizza Margherita

3 tablespoons olive oil
1 clove garlic, minced

1/2 teaspoon salt

1 1/2 pounds Roma tomatoes, thinly sliced

1/2 pound shredded mozzarella

1/4 cup packed basil leaves, torn by hand or cut in a chiffonade (tip, page 89)

Put the tomatoes in a shallow pan. Mix 2 tablespoons of the olive oil, garlic, and salt in a bowl and drizzle over the tomatoes. Let the tomatoes marinate for 10–15 minutes.

> Cookery means the economy of your grandmothers and the science of the modern chemist; it means much testing and no wasting; it means English thoroughness, French art, and Arabian hospitality.
> — Boston Cooking-School Cook Book (1896)

Brush the prebaked pizza crust with remaining 1 tablespoon olive oil. Add the tomatoes in an even layer and top with the shredded cheese. Bake for 5–7 minutes. Sprinkle with the basil as soon as it comes out of the oven.

Caramelized onion pizza

1/4 cup olive oil

3 pounds white onions, peeled and thinly sliced

1 garlic clove, minced

1 tablespoon fresh or 1/2 tablespoon dried thyme

salt, to taste

1/2 pound Gorgonzola cheese

Heat the oil in a large skillet over low heat. Add the onions, garlic, and thyme and stir to coat with the oil. Cover and cook, stirring occasionally, until the onions are soft and golden brown, approximately 45 minutes. Season with salt, to taste.

Spread the onion mixture on the prebaked pizza crust. Sprinkle the cheese evenly over the top. Bake for 7–8 minutes, until cheese is melty.

Roasted garlic, spinach, and feta pizza

1 whole head of garlic, unpeeled

3 tablespoons olive oil

1/4 large red onion, very finely minced

1 pound fresh spinach, washed, stemmed, and chopped

1 teaspoon salt

1 tablespoon balsamic vinegar

1/4 pound feta cheese, crumbled

ROAST THE GARLIC

Preheat oven to 400°F.

Cut off the top of the head of garlic about 1/4 inch from the top, exposing most of the cloves. Place garlic on a square of aluminum foil and drizzle with 1 tablespoon of the olive oil. Wrap the foil around the garlic, covering completely. Bake for 40–45 minutes, until soft to the touch. Let the bulb cool, then squeeze the soft garlic into a small bowl.

MAKE THE TOPPING

Heat 1 tablespoon olive oil in a large, lidded skillet over medium-low heat. Add the onion and cook for 1–2 minutes. Add the spinach, cover the pan, and cook for 3–5 minutes, until wilted. Stir in the vinegar and salt. Cook uncovered, stirring, for about 2 minutes more. If the spinach is very wet, transfer to a mesh strainer and press with a wooden spoon to remove excess liquid.

Brush the prebaked pizza crust with remaining 1 tablespoon olive oil. Spread the roasted garlic over the olive oil. Add the spinach in an even layer and top with the crumbled cheese. Bake for 5–7 minutes.

Mushroom and goat cheese pizza

3 tablespoons olive oil

1 pound fresh mushrooms, wiped clean with a damp towel and sliced

3 garlic cloves, minced

1/2 white onion, very thinly sliced

2 teaspoons minced fresh or 1 teaspoon dried rosemary

1/4 pound fresh goat cheese, crumbled

Heat 2 tablespoons olive oil in a large skillet. Add the mushrooms, garlic, and onions and sauté for 5–8 minutes. Drain any liquid from the pan.

Brush remaining 1 tablespoon of the olive oil on the prebaked crust. Top with the mushroom mixture. Sprinkle with the rosemary and cheese. Bake for 5–7 minutes.

White bean and green olive pizza

2 tablespoons olive oil

1/2 large white onion, chopped

3 cloves garlic, peeled and sliced

1/2 pound dry white beans, cannellini or Great Northern

1 tablespoon fresh or 1 1/2 teaspoons dried oregano + additional for garnish

157

6 cups vegetable broth

1/2 pound good-quality green olives, pitted and chopped

salt, to taste

Heat the olive oil over medium heat in a large stockpot. Add the onion and garlic and sauté until translucent. Add the beans, oregano, and broth and turn up the heat to medium-high. Bring to a boil, then reduce the heat to medium. Cover the pot and simmer until the beans are tender, about 2 hours.

Drain the beans in a colander, reserving the liquid. Puree the beans in a food processor, adding reserved liquid if needed to create a spreadable consistency. Season to taste with salt. Save the reserved seasoned broth for another use.

Skip the prebaking step and completely bake the pizza crust, 10–12 minutes total. Top the pizza with the white bean spread as soon as it comes out of the oven. Sprinkle the chopped olives on top. Garnish with additional oregano.

I SAY POTATO

My ethnic heritage is half Irish and half Polish, so a love for potatoes is baked into my

DNA. I can't think of a bad thing you can do to a potato.

Here are five tasty and easy ways to prepare tubers. Serve with a soup or salad, and you've got a complete vegetarian meal.

Casserole: Rosemary leek

2 cups milk

2 cups vegetable broth

3 cloves garlic, minced

1 tablespoon fresh or 1 teaspoon dried rosemary

1 bay leaf

3 pounds russet potatoes, scrubbed and thinly sliced

2 large leeks, thinly sliced (save tough upper leaves for soup stock)

salt and pepper, to taste

1 1/2 cups Swiss cheese

2 tablespoons butter + more for greasing the pan

Preheat oven to 375°F.

Generously grease a large baking pan with butter and set aside.

Combine milk, broth, garlic, rosemary, bay leaf, potatoes, and leeks in a large stockpot. Bring to a boil, and simmer about 10 minutes, until potatoes are just tender.

Place a colander in a large bowl. Drain the potatoes, discard the bay leaf, and reserve the cooking liquid.

Spread a single layer of potato and leek mixture in the prepared pan. Sprinkle with salt and pepper and a thin layer of cheese. Repeat layers until you run out of ingredients, ending with a layer of cheese. Pour reserved cooking liquid over potatoes until it reaches the top layer. (Any remaining liquid can be saved and used as a base for soup.)

Cut the butter into pieces and sprinkle over the casserole.

Bake until golden brown, about 1 hour.

Serves 4–6.

Pie: Mushroom and onion

2 large russet potatoes, peeled and sliced

2 cloves garlic, minced

1/4 cup milk, warmed

salt and pepper, to taste

3 tablespoons olive oil

1 large white onion, peeled and chopped

2 pounds fresh white or brown mushrooms, brushed clean and sliced

1/4 cup red wine

1/4 cup freshly grated Parmesan cheese

Preheat oven to 350°F.

Bring a large pot of salted water to a boil. Add potatoes and cook until tender but still firm, about 15 minutes. Drain potatoes, return them to the pot, and mash with the milk and garlic. Season with salt and pepper.

Heat 2 tablespoons olive oil in heavy lidded skillet over low heat. Add the onion and cook until translucent, about 5 minutes. Add the mushrooms and wine and cook until all of the liquid is absorbed, about 10–12 minutes.

Brush a 9-inch glass pie plate with remaining tablespoon of olive oil. Press the mashed potatoes into the pie plate, pressing up the sides to form a crust. Bake for 30 minutes.

Remove the crust from the oven and add the mushroom and onion mixture. Sprinkle with the cheese and bake for an additional 20 minutes.

Cool for 10 minutes before slicing and serving.

Pancakes: Sweet and spicy

2 sweet potatoes, scrubbed and shredded

2 russet potatoes, scrubbed and shredded

1 large white onion, peeled and quartered

2 eggs, lightly beaten

4 tablespoons all-purpose flour

2 teaspoons ground cinnamon

2 teaspoons ground cloves

2 teaspoons salt

vegetable oil for frying

Set aside half of the shredded sweet and russet potatoes in a large bowl.

Make the batter in two batches. In the bowl of a food processor, place half of the remaining potatoes, half of the onion, 1 egg, 2 tablespoons flour, 1 teaspoon cinnamon, 1 teaspoon cloves, and 1 teaspoon salt. Whirl it up to make a thick batter. Add the batter to the shredded potatoes, then process the remaining ingredients in the same way. Add the second batch of batter to the bowl, and stir all to combine.

Heat vegetable oil in a large skillet over medium-high heat. Test the oil by dropping in a few drops of water. If these sizzle and shake, it's ready. Pour batter in 3- or 4-inch rounds, and fry until golden on the bottom, about 2–3 minutes. Flip and fry the other side. Drain on paper-towel-topped newspapers or paper bags.

Continue frying the rest of the batter. Cooked pancakes can be kept warm in a low oven while you finish frying.

ROASTED: CARROT AND CHIVE

1/4 cup olive oil

2 1/2 pounds red-skinned potatoes, scrubbed and cubed

6 large carrots, scrubbed and cut into 3/4-inch pieces

2 large red onions, peeled, quartered, each quarter cut in half

1/4 cup balsamic vinegar

1/2 cup chopped fresh chives

salt and pepper, to taste

Preheat oven to 400°F.

Line a rimmed baking sheet with heavy aluminum foil. Pour the oil onto the foil-lined pan and coat evenly. Add the potatoes, carrots, and onions, and toss with a spatula to coat the veggies with the oil. Cover with foil and roast for 30 minutes.

Remove the foil and drizzle the veggies with the vinegar, tossing to coat. Continue roasting, uncovered, for another 30–40 minutes, until vegetables are browned and potatoes are crispy on the bottom, tossing 3–4 more times. Remove from the oven to a bowl and toss with the chopped chives.

Serves 4–6.

Baked: Red pepper and tomato

6 large russet potatoes, scrubbed

2 tablespoons olive oil

2 teaspoons kosher or sea salt

1 cup milk, warmed

4 tablespoons butter, softened

Red Pepper and Tomato Sauce (recipe follows)

salt and pepper, to taste

⅓ cup shredded Parmesan cheese

Preheat oven to 425°F.

Poke the potatoes a couple of times with a sharp knife or fork. Rub all over with the olive oil and salt. Bake until tender, about an hour.

Remove the potatoes from the oven and slice in half. Scoop out most of the pulp, leaving only a thin shell in the skin. Mash the potato pulp with the warm milk and butter. Add the Red Pepper and Tomato sauce and stir to blend completely. Season with salt and pepper.

Spoon the potato mixture back into the skins. Top with the shredded cheese and bake for another 10–15 minutes.

Serves 6.

Red Pepper and Tomato Sauce

1 red bell pepper, quartered and seeded

3 tablespoons olive oil

1/2 cup sun-dried tomatoes in oil

3 cloves garlic

Coat pepper quarters with 1 tablespoon of the olive oil. With the oven set to Broil, position a rack 2 inches from the flame and roast peppers for 15–18 minutes, turning once or twice. The skins should be black and blistered. Put the peppers in a paper bag and seal the top. When the peppers have cooled, slide the skins off with your fingers.

Place the peppers, tomatoes, garlic, and remaining 2 tablespoons olive oil in the bowl of a food processor and whirl into a sauce. Add a bit of warm water, red wine, or vegetable broth to thin if needed.

Fowl Play

Chickens are the backbone of the frugal

FRUGAL FOODIE TIP: AN A-PEELING IDEA!

Every year, my mom would clog the garbage disposer when she peeled the potatoes for Hanukkah latkes. It was as much a tradition as candles and gelt. We thought it was just a quirk of her sink, but recently I read that grinding potato peels in the disposer turns them into a mashed-potato-like mass that's almost guaranteed to clog your drains.

An easy solution is to line your sink with newspaper, peel the potatoes into the paper, and then chuck the whole thing in your compost heap or trash.

kitchen. Less expensive than beef or pork, and useful down to the bones.

The most frugal way to use chickens is to buy them whole and cut them up yourself. You'll not only save money, but chicken tastes much better when cooked with the skin and bones. A whole, organic bird usually costs less per pound than precut, skinned, and boned parts, and it tastes so much better.

Cooking with *Confit*-dence

I first heard the term *confit* on an episode of the 1980s PBS cooking show *The Frugal Gourmet*. The affable and not-yet-disgraced host, Jeff Smith, earnestly pronounced it with a quasi-French accent that was straight out of Monty Python. It became a family joke for years.

Confit (cohn-FEE) is a classic French cooking method in which food is slow-cooked in its own fat. It's a cheap trick used by restaurants to make the food taste extra rich and delicious. Once you've mastered the technique, try it with duck or turkey and experiment with different herbs.

Garlic chicken confit

6 whole chicken leg quarters

1/4 cup olive oil

1 head of garlic, cloves separated and peeled

sprigs of fresh rosemary, thyme, or oregano

salt and pepper, to taste

Preheat oven to 225°F.

Place chicken leg quarters snugly in a single layer in a large roasting pan. Place a rimmed baking sheet under the roasting pan to catch any overflow of juices. Nestle the garlic cloves among the chicken pieces and tuck in the fresh herbs. Sprinkle with salt and pepper. Drizzle with the olive oil.

Bake the chicken for about an hour. Check the pan. If it has spilled over or looks as if it's about to, skim off some of the liquid fat.

Turn the heat up to 350°F and cook until chicken skin is golden brown. Remove from the oven and allow to cool in the fat for 15–20 minutes.

To serve immediately, remove the chicken from the fat and blot on paper towels, or pull the meat from the bones and shred it to serve over pasta or salad greens. Reserve the skin and bones for making soup stock.

To store, put the whole legs or shredded meat in an airtight container and cover with the liquid fat. Store in the fridge for a week, or up to 6 months in the freezer. To reheat, sauté in a few tablespoons of the reserved fat until crisp and golden.

Exponential Chicken

This amazing bird multiplies to feed two people for 5 days. The concept was inspired by, of all things, *The Newlywed Game*. When I was a kid I saw an episode in which a young couple proudly declared that the only thing they had for dinner was turkey. The wife cooked a turkey on Sunday, and they ate off that bird all week. This made a big impression on me. The scheme struck me as elegant in its simplicity, and horrifying in its monotony.

My take on the weeklong bird is to poach a whole chicken on Sunday and create a week's worth of tasty and varied meals.

1 whole roaster chicken, 5–6 pounds

2 celery stalks, cut into 2-inch pieces

2 large carrots, cut into 2-inch pieces

1 large onion, peeled and quartered

1 bay leaf

1/2 lemon

1 bunch parsley

Put all of the ingredients into a large stockpot with a tight-fitting lid. Fill with enough water to cover the chicken by 2 inches. Bring to a boil over high heat. Lower the heat to medium and simmer for 20 minutes, skimming off any schmutz that forms at the top.

Cover the pot and turn off the heat. Let the chicken steep in the hot liquid for 1 1/2 hours.

Remove the chicken from the pot, letting the broth drain back into the pot. Let the chicken cool completely on a cutting board.

Put a colander over another stockpot or large bowl and pour the contents of the stockpot into it to strain out the vegetables. Cool the broth to room temperature on the stove top, then put in the fridge. When the broth has cooled, skim off the fat and reserve, and store the broth in an airtight container.

Once the chicken has cooled, remove the meat from the bones. First remove the whole breasts and store them in foil. Shred the leg and thigh meat with your hands and reserve it in an airtight container. Store the skin and bones in a heavy-duty plastic bag.

Dinner 1: Chicken Curry

1/2 tablespoon vegetable oil

1/2 tablespoon butter

1/2 large onion, peeled and thinly sliced

2 cloves garlic, minced

1 tablespoon fresh cilantro or 1 teaspoon ground coriander

1 tablespoon curry powder

2 Roma tomatoes, chopped

1 small green chile pepper, such as jalapeño, seeded and thinly sliced

1/4 cup water

1 poached chicken breast half, cut into 1-inch cubes

Melt the oil and butter in a large skillet over medium-low heat. Add the onions and cook until very soft and golden, stirring often, about 30 minutes.

Add the garlic and sauté for another 2 minutes. Add the cilantro or coriander, curry powder, tomatoes, chile, and water and stir to combine. Simmer for 5 minutes. Add the cooked chicken and simmer for another 10 minutes.

Serve over rice.

Dinner 2: Tacos Naranjas

1/2 tablespoon vegetable oil

1/2 tablespoon butter

1/2 large onion, peeled and thinly sliced

2 cloves garlic, minced

3/4 cup orange juice

1/4 teaspoon ground cumin

1 jalapeño pepper, seeded and sliced

1 poached chicken breast half, shredded

Melt the oil and butter in a large skillet over medium-low heat. Add the onions and cook until translucent. Add the garlic and sauté for another 2 minutes. Add the orange juice, cumin, and jalapeño and simmer for 5 minutes. Add the shredded chicken and simmer until the liquid is absorbed, about 10–15 minutes.

Serve with shredded lettuce in warm tortillas.

Dinner 3: Matzo Ball Soup

1 egg, slightly beaten

1 tablespoon chicken fat, melted

1/4 cup matzo meal

1/4 teaspoon salt

dash of pepper

1 large carrot, scrubbed and thinly sliced.

reserved chicken broth (save 1 cup for the paella, page 174)

Blend the egg with the melted chicken fat in a small bowl with a fork. Add the matzo meal, salt, and pepper and mix thoroughly. Chill for 30 minutes.

Place the reserved chicken broth and sliced carrot in a soup pot and bring to a boil. With wet hands, form the matzo ball mixture into walnut-sized balls. Drop them into the boiling soup, then reduce the heat to medium, cover the pot, and simmer for 20 minutes. Season with salt and pepper.

Dinner 4: Pretty Close to Paella

1 tablespoon olive oil

1 garlic clove, chopped

1/2 large white onion, finely chopped

1/2 green pepper, seeded and cut into strips

1 large hot sausage, sliced into 12 pieces

1/2 cup long-grain white rice

1/2 cup white wine

2 cups chicken broth

1 pinch saffron threads

1/4 pound shrimp, whole in the shell

half of the reserved leg and thigh meat from the poached chicken

1/2 cup small pimiento-stuffed green olives, sliced

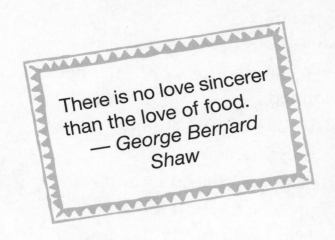

There is no love sincerer than the love of food.
— George Bernard Shaw

Preheat oven to 400°F.

Heat oil in a 12-inch heavy skillet over high heat until it glistens. Sauté garlic and onion and pepper strips, stirring, until garlic and onion are golden, about 2 minutes. Add sausage and cook, stirring, until it is lightly browned, about 2 minutes. Add rice, wine, broth, saffron, shrimp, and chicken and stir well. Put the pan in the oven and cook for 25 minutes, or until liquid is absorbed. Stir in olives.

Dinner 5: Almond Soup

reserved skin and bones from poached chicken

4 cups water

1 bay leaf

1 tablespoon olive oil

1/2 large white onion, peeled and chopped

2 garlic cloves, peeled and minced

1/2 cup white wine

1/4 teaspoon ground cumin

1/4 cup blanched almonds

remaining half of the leg and thigh meat from the poached chicken

salt and pepper, to taste

Place the skin, bones, water, and bay leaf in a saucepan. Bring to a boil. Reduce heat and simmer for 20 minutes. Strain out the skin, bones, and bay leaf, returning the broth to the pan.

In a small skillet, heat the olive oil over medium-low heat. Add the onion and garlic and cook, stirring, until the onion is translucent. Add the wine and cumin and cook for 5 minutes. Working in batches, place the onion mixture, broth, and almonds in a blender or food processor and process until smooth. Put the pureed soup back into the saucepan over medium heat. Add the chicken and cook until just heated through.

Hard-Boiled Curry in a Hurry

Which came first, the chicken or the egg? We'll never know, but when you've started your week with chicken dinners, you can end it with this yummy take on Indian curry.

12 eggs

1 tablespoon salt

2 large russet potatoes, peeled and cut into 1-inch pieces

3 tablespoons curry powder

1 teaspoon ground coriander

1 tablespoon cider vinegar

2 tablespoons vegetable oil

2 tablespoons butter

1 large white onion, peeled and chopped

6 garlic cloves, peeled and sliced

4 Roma tomatoes, chopped — keep the seeds and juice

1/4 cup fresh cilantro leaves, chopped, for garnish

Bring a large pot of water to a boil. Add the eggs and boil for 10 minutes. Remove the eggs with a slotted spoon and set aside to cool.

Add the salt to the water, stirring, then add the potatoes. Cook until the potatoes are tender, about 5 minutes. Drain in a colander. When the eggs are cool to the touch, peel and chop them into bite-sized chunks.

In a small bowl, mix the curry powder, coriander, and cider vinegar. Set aside.

Heat the oil and butter in a skillet over medium-low heat. Add the onion and garlic and cook for 5 minutes. Add the spice mixture and tomatoes and cook, stirring, for 5 minutes. Add the chopped eggs and the potatoes and toss to coat. Reduce heat to low, cover the pan, and simmer for 5 minutes. Add a little warm water or chicken broth if the curry looks too dry. Season with salt and pepper.

Serve over steamed white rice garnished with cilantro.

Serves 6.

Retro Date-Night Restaurant Dinners

I've got a soft spot for old-school 50s and 60s "chop house"-style restaurants. The kinds of places with relish trays, tufted red banquettes, and Thousand Island dressing for your iceberg-lettuce-and-cherry-tomato salad. The kind of place Don and Betty Draper from the television series *Mad Men* might go on a date night in Ossining.

> There is no spectacle on earth more appealing than that of a beautiful woman in the act of cooking dinner for someone she loves.
> — Thomas Wolfe

While these joints are fewer and farther between today, and the cuisine has given way to more modern fare, I love the idea of recreating your own retro date-night dinners at home. Create an entire experience with starched white tablecloths, mesh-bagged candleholders, and Louis Prima on the stereo.

Steak au Poivre

Brandy or Cognac is a bit of a splurge, but you can cut the expense by using a minibottle. If you don't have upcoming travel plans, you can find these bottles at most large liquor stores.

1 large tenderloin steak, 1 inch thick, about

10 ounces

1/2 tablespoon kosher salt

1/2 tablespoon whole black peppercorns

1/2 tablespoon olive oil

3 shallots, finely chopped

4 tablespoons butter, cut into 4 pieces

1 minibottle ("airplane mini") of brandy or Cognac

1/4 cup heavy cream

salt and pepper, to taste

Crush the peppercorns with a mortar and pestle; or place them in a pie plate and whack with a meat tenderizer; or place them in a ziplock bag and whack with a heavy skillet. Sprinkle the kosher salt on both sides of the steak, and press the crushed peppercorns into the steak. Let it rest at room temperature for at least an hour before cooking.

Heat the oil in a heavy skillet over high heat. Add the steak and cook medium rare, about 5 minutes on each side. Remove the steak to a platter and keep in a low (200°F) oven while you finish the sauce.

Pour off the fat from the pan. Melt 2 tablespoons of butter in the pan and add the shallots. Cook for 3–5 minutes, scraping the browned bits from the bottom of the pan. Add the Cognac or brandy and boil for 2–3 minutes. The liquor may ignite — high drama! — but just shake the pan a bit until the flames die down.

Reduce the heat to medium and add the cream and any juices that have puddled in the platter under the steak. Bring to a boil and cook until the sauce is thick enough to coat the back of a spoon, about 5 minutes. Remove from the heat and add the remaining 2 tablespoons butter, stirring to melt and blend.

Pour the sauce over the steak, and serve.

Scampi without Skimping

1/2 cup olive oil

1/2 pound large, uncooked, unpeeled shrimp (if you can get them with the heads on, even better)

1 large carrot, scrubbed and cut into 1-inch pieces

1 rib of celery, washed and cut into 1-inch pieces

1/2 large white onion, peeled and quartered

4 large garlic cloves, peeled and sliced

3/4 cup white wine

1 tablespoon olive oil

2 tablespoons butter

juice of 1 small lemon

dash of red pepper flakes

1/2 pound thin pasta — capellini, spaghetti, or linguine

1/4 cup chopped flat-leaf parsley

Remove the shells from the shrimp and place them in a large saucepan with the carrot, celery, onion, and half of the garlic. Add the wine and bring to a boil. Boil until the liquid is reduced by half, about 5–8 minutes. Strain the shells and veggies and reserve the cooking liquid.

Cut each of the shrimp into 3 pieces.

Preheat a skillet over medium heat, then add the butter and oil and stir until butter is melted. Add the remaining garlic and cook for 3 minutes. Add the shrimp and cook until they are pink. Add the reserved cooking liquid, lemon juice, and red pepper flakes and cook for 3–4 minutes more.

Serve over al dente capellini, spaghetti, or linguine, garnished with chopped parsley.

Stuffed Pork Chops

2 pork chops, bone-in, 1 inch thick

1 cup water

1/2 teaspoon salt

2 tablespoons olive oil

1/4 large white onion, finely chopped

1/2 tart green apple, peeled, cored, and finely chopped

1 cup dried bread cubes

3/4 cup white wine

2 teaspoons fresh or 1/2 teaspoon dried sage

2 teaspoons stone-ground mustard

1 tablespoon butter

Preheat oven to 400°F.

A good cook is like a sorceress who dispenses happiness.
— Elsa Schiaparelli

Remove the bones from the pork chops. Place the bones in a shallow pan and roast for 30 minutes. Put the roasted bones in a small saucepan and add the water and salt. Bring the water to a boil. Boil until the liquid is reduced by half, about 10–15 minutes. Strain the broth and reserve, discarding the bones.

Heat 1 tablespoon olive oil in a large skillet over medium heat. Add the onion and apple and cook for 5 minutes. Add the bread cubes and reserved pork broth; stir to coat. Cover the pan and let the stuffing sit for 10 minutes.

With a sharp knife, cut a slit in each pork chop, making a deep pocket. Fill the pockets with the stuffing.

In a heavy ovenproof skillet (preferably cast iron), heat the remaining 1 tablespoon olive oil over medium-high heat and brown the pork chops, about 3 minutes on each side. Add the wine, cover, and reduce heat to medium. Simmer for 8–10 minutes. Remove the chops from the pan and keep warm.

Add the sage and mustard to the pan sauce, stirring to combine. Increase the heat to high and cook for 5 minutes, scraping any browned bits from the bottom of the pan. Remove from heat and stir in the butter.

Pour sauce over chops, and serve.

FRUGAL FOODIE TIP: INSTANT GRANITAFICATION

Freeze fruit juice or leftover sweetened coffee in an ice cube tray. Fit your food processor with the shredder disk and press the cubes through the feeder tube. Pile the sweet "snow" in wine glasses. One full tray of cubes makes 4 servings.

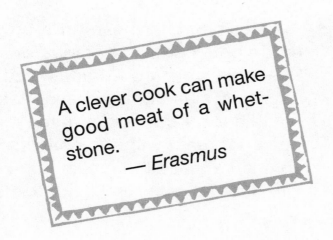

A clever cook can make good meat of a whetstone.
— *Erasmus*

PLEASED TO MEAT YOU!

Leg and shoulder "value" cuts are very flavorful and cost less than steaks and chops.

The American Meat Institute recommends these methods for tenderizing value cuts of meat:

- Marinate less tender cuts of meat in a liquid containing an acid such as vinegar, wine, or lemon or lime juice. As the meat stands in the liquid, the acid breaks down the tough muscle fibers. The formula for liquid to meat is 1/2 cup of liquid per 1 pound of meat. Since marinades only penetrate about 1/4 inch into meats, it is key to use a cut that is relatively thin.
- Always marinate meats in a covered container in the refrigerator. Use a sealable food-grade plastic bag or a glass or stainless steel container so the acidic marinade does not react with the container. To ensure that all the meat comes into contact with the liquid, use a

container that is just large enough to hold the meat.

- If some of the marinade is to be used as a sauce on the cooked meat, reserve a portion of the marinade before adding the raw meat. Or rapidly boil used marinade to destroy any harmful bacteria before adding it to cooked meats. Otherwise, discard the leftover marinade and do not add it to any other foods.
- Pound steaks with the flat side of a meat mallet. Pound from the center of the steak to the edges.
- Score steaks or roasts with a sharp knife. Make diagonal shallow cuts across the surface to cut the long muscle fibers.
- Use low heat and a moist-cooking method to soften the connective tissues that run through the muscles. Both slow cooking and braising are perfect cooking techniques for value cuts.
- Holding a sharp knife at an angle away from you, slice roasts and

steaks across the grain, on the diagonal, into very thin slices. Slicing across the grain shortens the long muscle fibers and results in a more tender product. This procedure is beneficial as a final tenderizing technique for cutting raw meat for stir-fry recipes and carving cooked meats.

— from *Meat Matters: Stretch Your Meat Dollar,* published by the American Meat Institute

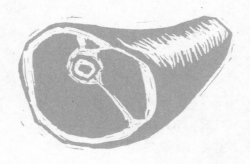

CENTS-ABLE SOLUTIONS:
SAVVY SUBSTITUTIONS

You know that every time you run out to the store for "just one thing" you end up with several more items in your bag, and several fewer dollars in your wallet. You'll spare yourself these spendy trips to the store when you can draw on an arsenal of savvy subs for common ingredients.

On one occasion, I wanted to make my friend's delicious rice salad. It called for a relatively small amount of basil, and I couldn't find it at the closest market. I was a less confident cook back then, and as faithful to a written recipe as Moses was to the Ten Commandments. I hit three more stores — still no basil, and I was burning gas at a fast clip. I finally found some at the organic superstore. I paid through the nose, but by then I was desperate. When I recounted my tale to my pal on the phone, she said, "Oh, I make it with parsley all the time when I don't have basil. It's just as good." I could have saved a lot of time, money, and grief if I'd trusted my instincts and done a switch-a-roo.

ITEM	SAVVY SUB
baking powder (1 teaspoon)	1/4 teaspoon baking soda + 1/4 teaspoon cream of tartar
buttermilk (1 cup)	1 tablespoon white vinegar + milk to equal 1 cup. Let stand 5 minutes
capers	green olives, finely chopped
chocolate, unsweetened	3 tablespoons cocoa powder + 1 tablespoon olive oil
corn syrup (light)	1 cup sugar + 1/4 cup water
currants or dates	raisins
cream of tartar (1 teaspoon)	1 teaspoon white vinegar
fish sauce	soy sauce mixed with anchovy paste
cake flour (1 cup)	1 cup less 2 tablespoons all-purpose flour

self-rising four (1 cup)	1 cup all-purpose flour + 1 1/2 teaspoons baking powder and a dash of salt
molasses	3/4 cup brown sugar dissolved in 1/4 cup warm water
maple syrup	Bring 1 cup water and 1 tablespoon butter to a boil. Add 1/2 cup sugar and 1 cup brown sugar, stirring to dissolve. Simmer for 3–4 minutes and add 1 tablespoon of butter.
mustard (dry) 1 teaspoon	1 tablespoon prepared mustard
oil	Replace oil in baked goods with mashed bananas or applesauce.
sesame oil	2 teaspoons sesame seeds sautéed in 1/4 cup vegetable oil
shallots	scallions (white part only)

sugar, superfine	equal amount of granulated sugar pulsed in a food processor for 30–40 seconds
sugar, brown (1 cup)	1 cup granulated sugar + 3 tablespoons molasses
sugar, powdered (1 cup)	1 cup granulated sugar + 1 teaspoon cornstarch finely ground in a food processor
wine, red	beef broth
wine, white	chicken broth

Chapter 6
Pulled-Purse-Strings Parties

Entertaining doesn't have to be draining — on your nerves or your pocketbook — and it doesn't have to mean you're putting on a show for your guests. A delicious meal and good conversation is all you need for a lovely, cheap evening's entertainment.

One of my favorite entertainers is fashion designer, media gadfly, and all-around bon vivant Isaac Mizrahi. On his all-too-short-lived cable talk show, he and his guests chatted while engaging in activities, rather than sitting across from each other at a desk. He shopped with Kristin Davis, played Ping-Pong with Jonathan Adler, and knitted with

193

Pull up a chair. Take a taste. Come join us. Life is so endlessly delicious.

— Ruth Reichl

Janeane Garofalo. The idea was that his guests felt more comfortable and chatted more easily when they were doing something. I wholeheartedly agree.

Engaging your guests in some aspect of the meal prep — bringing an ingredient, rolling out pasta dough, whipping cream for dessert — brings them closer, encourages conversation, and helps spread out the outlay of time and money.

PASTA ROLL PLAY

Making, kneading, rolling, and cutting pasta is a fun, easy, and unique way to start off a dinner party. Pour some wine, pass some light nibbles, and have a few old T-shirts around to use as smocks to protect your guests' clothes from puffs of flour.

Dough (for Not Much Dough)

2 1/2 cups flour

3 large eggs, room temperature

2 teaspoons olive oil

Pinch of salt

Make a mountain of flour in the middle of a large wooden cutting board. Make a well in the top of the mountain and put the eggs, oil, and salt in it.

Beat the eggs with a fork, then gradually start to bring in the flour and continue beating with the fork. Once the egg mixture is pretty thick, gently incorporate the rest of the flour with your hands, until the dough forms a ball. If the dough is sticky, add a little more flour. If it's dry, add a teaspoon of water.

Knead the dough until it is smooth and elastic, about 5 minutes. Cover the dough with a bowl and let it rest for 30 minutes.

Divide the dough into 4 pieces. On a floured surface, roll one section into a long rectangle. With a sharp knife, cut the dough into thin ribbons. Repeat with the rest of the dough.

Cook fresh pasta in lots (at least 5 quarts)

of boiling salted water. Don't skimp on the salt. Add all of the fresh pasta to the water at the same time. Stir the pasta while it cooks. It will be ready in as little as 90 seconds.

Reserve 1/2 cup of the cooking liquid — this can be used to adjust the thickness of the sauce — and drain the pasta.

Makes about 1 pound of dough, or enough pasta for 6 main-course servings.

Pennywise Pasta Sauce

Classic carbonara sauce uses a stingy pit of smoked pork (pancetta or bacon) and lots of thrifty eggs to create a luxuriously creamy sauce.

3 large eggs

1/2 teaspoon salt

1/4 pound Parmesan cheese, grated

1/4 cup chopped flat-leaf parsley

2 tablespoons olive oil

1/4 pound pancetta or bacon, sliced into 1/2-inch pieces

1 medium white onion, chopped

1/2 cup white wine

In a small bowl, whisk the eggs, salt, cheese, and parsley and set aside.

Everything you see I owe to spaghetti.
— Sophia Loren

Heat the olive oil in a large skillet over medium heat. Add the bacon and onion and cook for 5–7 minutes. The bacon should cook through, but not get crispy. Add the wine and cook for 5 minutes, stirring and scraping the bottom of the pan. Remove the pan from the heat.

Add the cooked, drained pasta to the pan and toss to coat with the bacon and sauce. Add the egg mixture and, working quickly, toss to coat completely. Add reserved pasta cooking liquid a tablespoon at a time as needed to create a silky sauce.

Co-Op Coppa di Frutta

Ask each of your guests to bring a different type of fruit to contribute to this easy trifle.

FRUGAL FOODIE TIP: TRYING DRYING

You can dry fresh pasta for longer storage. An easy way to dry long strands is on the top rack of your oven. Remove the lower racks and hang the pasta through the wires of the top rack. Make sure to put a note on your oven — or remove the knob — to make sure it doesn't get turned on while the pasta is drying.

Make the pound cake, lemon curd, and whipped cream before guests arrive, and assemble the trifle as the fruit appears. Store the dessert in the fridge while you have dinner, to give the flavors time to develop.

POUND CAKE

2 sticks unsalted butter, room temperature

1 cup granulated sugar

1 teaspoon vanilla extract

4 large eggs, room temperature

2 cups all-purpose flour

1 teaspoon baking powder

1 teaspoon salt

Preheat oven to 325°F.

Generously butter a 5-inch x 9-inch loaf pan.

In a large bowl, cream the butter, sugar, and vanilla with an electric mixer, until light and fluffy. Add the eggs one at a time, mixing to combine after each addition. Add the flour, baking powder, and salt and mix in on low speed until just combined.

Scrape the batter into the prepared pan. Bake for about an hour and give it a check. The top should be golden and a skewer or butter knife stuck in the middle should come out clean.

Cool in the pan on a rack for 10–15 minutes. Run a knife or flat spatula around the outside of the cake and turn it out onto the rack to cool completely.

LEMON CURD

6 egg yolks

3/4 cup sugar

grated zest of 1 lemon

3/4 cup fresh lemon juice

2 teaspoons cornstarch

2 teaspoons water

Whisk the egg yolks, sugar, zest, and juice in a stainless steel bowl. Set the bowl over a pan of simmering water and whisk until the mixture begins to thicken, 4–5 minutes.

Mix the cornstarch and water in a small bowl and add to the curd. Continue cooking and stirring until the mixture is thick, about 5 minutes. (It will continue to thicken as it cools.)

Transfer the curd to a glass bowl and cover with plastic wrap directly on the curd. Chill in the fridge.

WHIPPED CREAM

1 pint heavy whipping cream

2 tablespoons confectioners' sugar

Chill a metal bowl and mixer beaters for at least 30 minutes before whipping the cream. Shake the container of whipping cream well and pour it into the mixing bowl. Starting on medium speed, whip the cream until it begins to thicken. Increase the speed to high and gradually add in the sugar. Continue beating until stiff peaks form.

TO FINISH THE TRIFLE

3–4 cups fresh fruit, such as berries, peaches, pears, plums, and bananas, washed or peeled and chopped into bite-sized bits

4 tablespoons rum, brandy, or any fruit liqueur

As soon as your guests arrive, set one of them to cutting the pound cake into crouton-sized cubes.

In a large glass bowl, layer the ingredients, starting with the cake cubes. Sprinkle with a tablespoon of liqueur. Spread a layer of lemon curd, then a layer of whipped cream, then a layer of fruit.

Continue layering until all of the ingredients are used up.

Keep the trifle in the fridge until ready to
serve.

GET PUNCHY

A big bowl or pitcher of a signature drink is
much more economical than a full bar, and
it stretches your booze dollar.

Café Cocktail

6 cups cold coffee

1 cup heavy cream

1 cup coffee-flavored liqueur, such as Kahlúa

ground nutmeg

Mix all of the ingredients in a pitcher or punch bowl. Serve over ice, with a shake of nutmeg on top.

Makes 8 1-cup servings.

Savers Sangría

2 large oranges, thinly sliced

2 large lemons, thinly sliced

1/2 cup orange-flavored liqueur

1/2 cup orange juice

2 bottles cheap red wine, chilled

2 10-ounce bottles berry-flavored sparkling water, chilled

Mix first five ingredients in a large bowl. Just before serving, add the sparking water. Serve in ice-filled glasses.

Makes about 12 3/4-cup servings.

Pomegranate Warm-Up

1 cup pomegranate juice

2 oranges, sliced

1/2 teaspoon ground nutmeg

12 whole cloves

4 cinnamon sticks

2 cups sugar

1 1/4 cups water

2 bottles cheap red wine

Put all ingredients in a large stockpot and bring to a simmer over low heat. Simmer for 20–30 minutes; do not let the mixture boil. Strain fruit and spices from the punch and return it to the stockpot. Serve from the stove top in coffee mugs.

Makes about 8 1-cup servings.

Stone Soup

In the classic Stone Soup tale, a group of hungry travelers arrive in town with nothing but a large pot and a small stone. They put the stone in a pot of water over a fire in the middle of the square and crow to all who pass by about the delicious Stone Soup that only needs "a little something." The townsfolk are all willing to spare a bit of what they have — a potato, an onion, some spices — until the pot is brimming with a hearty soup that can feed the entire village.

Your Stone Soup party doesn't have to be as sneaky — but everyone at the table can contribute to the meal.

FRUGAL FOODIE TIP: GET STONED!

Heat a clean, wide, flat stone in a 250°F oven for 15 minutes. Put it in the bottom of your breadbasket, then line with a cloth napkin and fill with bread. It will keep your bread warm on the table.

Block Party Bouillabaisse

Ask each guest to bring a cup of seafood to add to the pot.

1/2 cup white wine

pinch of saffron threads

2 tablespoons olive oil

2 cloves garlic, peeled and smashed

1 large onion, peeled and sliced

1 small fennel bulb, thinly sliced

1 strip orange zest

2 large tomatoes, chopped, including seeds and juice

6 cups clam juice

6 cups seafood, including some or all of the following: halibut, cod, tilapia, snapper, large shrimp (uncooked, unpeeled), lump crabmeat, clams, or mussels

1 bunch flat-leaf parsley, chopped

lemon wedges

Heat the wine in a small saucepan or in the microwave until very warm. Add the saffron threads and set aside.

Heat the olive oil in a large skillet over medium heat. Add the garlic, onion, and fennel and sauté until tender and lightly browned, about 7 minutes. Add the wine and saffron, orange zest, tomatoes, and clam juice. Bring to a boil and cook until the liquid is reduced by half, about 15–20 minutes.

Reduce heat to medium and add the fish, but not the shellfish. Simmer for 3 minutes. Add the shellfish and cook for 4–5 minutes longer, until shells have opened. Add any crabmeat and stir into the stew. Cook 2–3 minutes to heat through. Sprinkle with parsley and serve with a wedge or two of lemon.

Bowled-Over Chili

Each guest can bring a small round loaf of bread to use as a chili bowl. Extra bonus: fewer dishes to wash!

3 cups dried beans, one or more of black, pinto, or kidney

2 tablespoons olive oil

1 pound ground pork butt

1 large onion, peeled and diced

3 cloves garlic, minced

1 large bell pepper, cored, seeded, and diced

2 large carrots, scrubbed and diced

1 cup fresh corn kernels (from about 2 ears)

1 tablespoon flour

1 tablespoon cornmeal

1 1/2 cups beef broth

2 6-ounce cans tomato paste

6 large fresh tomatoes, diced, including seeds and juice

2 fresh jalapeño chiles, seeded and sliced

CHILI SEASONINGS

1 tablespoon chili powder

1 tablespoon ground cumin

2 teaspoons dried oregano

1/2 teaspoon red pepper flakes

1 tablespoon brown sugar

1/8 teaspoon cayenne pepper

2 teaspoons salt

1/2 teaspoon freshly ground pepper

The night before you plan to serve the chili, pick through the beans and remove any pebbles or funky-looking beans.

Place the beans in a large stockpot. Fill the pot with water to cover by about 2 inches. Let the beans soak overnight.

The next day, drain the beans, rinse them, and return them to the pot. Fill the pot with fresh water to cover by 2 inches. Bring the water to a boil. Reduce heat to medium and simmer until tender, about an hour. Drain the beans and return them to the pot.

Mix the chili seasonings in a medium bowl and set aside.

Heat the olive oil in a large skillet over medium heat. Add the pork to the pan and cook through, about 5–10 minutes. Add the onion, garlic, bell pepper, carrots, corn, flour, and cornmeal, and cook until the onion is browned, about 5–7 minutes. Whisk the broth and tomato paste into the chili seasoning mix until combined, and add to the meat and veggie mixture. Simmer the sauce for 10 minutes.

Add the chili sauce to the beans and mix well to combine. Add the chopped tomatoes and jalapeños. Simmer the chili for 10–15 minutes, until it is thick and heated through.

Makes 8–10 servings.

Legendary Stone Soup

Relive the story by asking each guest to contribute a veggie or some noodles to the soup.

- 1 1/2 tablespoons butter
- 1 1/2 tablespoons olive oil
- 1 large onion, peeled and diced
- 2 1/2 large garlic cloves, minced
- 2 1/2 tablespoons flour
- 8 cups chicken or vegetable broth

SUGGESTED CONTRIBUTIONS

- 2 celery stalks, scrubbed, trimmed, and thinly sliced
- 2 large carrots, scrubbed and thinly sliced
- 4 medium red-skinned potatoes, scrubbed and cubed

1 large zucchini or yellow squash, diced

1 bunch spinach, rinsed and chopped

1 cup dried small pasta such as orzo or macaroni, cooked al dente

salt and freshly ground black pepper, to taste

Almond and Arugula Pesto (recipe follows)

In a large stockpot, melt the butter with the olive oil over medium heat. Add the onion and garlic and sauté for 5 minutes. Sprinkle the flour over the veggies and cook, stirring, for 2–3 minutes. Add the broth and bring to a boil. Reduce the heat to low and keep it simmering.

As your guests arrive, toss their contributions into the broth. Simmer for 15–20 minutes. Serve topped with a dollop of pesto.

Almond and Arugula Pesto

1/4 cup raw almonds, toasted (see page 75)

2 large cloves garlic, peeled

1/2 cup fresh arugula leaves, packed

1/4 cup grated Parmesan cheese

1/2 cup olive oil

salt, to taste

Place all of the ingredients in the bowl of a food processor and whirl to combine. Season with more salt, if needed.

I still think that one of the pleasantest of all emotions is to know that I, I with my brain and my hands, have nourished my beloved few, that I have concocted a stew or a story, a rarity or a plain dish, to sustain them truly against the hungers of the world. — M.F.K. Fisher

CENTS-ABLE SOLUTIONS:
"ANTIDEPRESSANTS"

No, not the kind that come in bottles pre-scribed by Dr. Feelgood. These antide-pressants are the rules, tips, and strate-gies that our parents, grandparents, and great-grandparents used to survive the Great Depression. My great-grandma Mimi used and reused tea bags and saved rainwater for her houseplants de-cades after the depression ended, even when she could well afford not to. While we may roll our eyes at some of the more eccentric quirks (my great-grandpa Dave saved every pen and rubber band he came across), there are many valuable lessons to be learned from those who have faced truly hard times.

- Learn to do simple mending and al-terations. Your clothes will last lon-ger, and if you find clothing on sale that needs a nip or a tuck, you'll be able to do it yourself.

- Reuse everything. Old shirts make great nightshirts and smocks. Old nightshirts and smocks make great rags.
- Keep your bread in the freezer. It will keep for weeks and weeks without getting stale or moldy, and defrosts quickly on the countertop or in a toaster oven.
- You really can reuse tea bags for a second cup of tea. After that, let them cool and use them as a soothing eye mask.
- When you've finished your coffee and want just one more cup, don't make a whole pot. Just run half as much water as you used for a full pot back through the grounds.
- Free fun: Play board games and Charades and have homemade treasure hunts instead of going out to the movies.
- Ditch the car once in a while — walk to the store, school, or library. What was once a quick errand can turn into an afternoon adventure.
- "If you can't afford to pay cash, you

can't afford it." Cut up all but one emergency credit card. Go to the grocery store with cash instead of a credit card. A study by Visa showed that customers who shopped with credit cards spent 30 percent more than those who spent cash.

- Buy in bulk. You'll save lots on items that store well, such as rice, grains, and beans.
- I'll trade ya! Barter with friends and neighbors for everything from babysitting to car repairs. You can also find barter buddies on Craigslist: www.craigslist.com.
- Before you buy something new, see if you can learn how to fix it yourself. Check the manufacturer's website for the owner's manual if you no longer have it, and check the library for household repair books. If an appliance is beyond repair, give it to your kids with a couple of screwdrivers — they'll love to play "Take Apart."
- Frugal doesn't mean cheap! Be

generous with your time, skills, and as much money as you can.

- Save for rainy days. Pay into your savings account before you pay for anything else.
- When you do need to buy something, think preowned before new. Kids' shoes and clothing at thrift stores and resale shops have lots of wear left in them, and designer duds can be had for pennies on the dollar. Try looking in shops in upscale neighborhoods. Rich folks' homes are full of preowned furniture. They call them "antiques" and "heirlooms," but your yard sale finds can look just as good.
- Buy for function, not fashion. A $20 watch tells the same time as a $200 watch.
- Keep a scrap bag in the freezer. Throw in vegetable peels and bits of meat and bones. When the bag is full, simmer the scraps in salted water for an hour and you'll have a tasty broth to use in recipes.

- Use a butter wrapper to grease pans.
- Shopping is not entertainment. If you're bored or antsy, pick up a book, go to the library, or work on a craft project. As my Aunt Ruthy says about her knitting hobby, "It keeps me out of the stores."
- When the shampoo or conditioner has run out, fill the bottle half full with water and give it a shake. You'll get several more uses out of the product.
- In the winter, turn down the thermostat and put on a sweater. In the summer, cool off with cold drinks and fans instead of air conditioning.
- Wash all your laundry in cold water. Your clothes will be perfectly clean and will last longer. Dry your clothes on a clothesline.
- Use cloth napkins and dishrags instead of paper.
- Learn to cut up a chicken. Whole chickens are much cheaper than parts.

- Cut off the tops of gallon jugs and put them outside when it rains to collect water for watering house-plants and gardens.
- Understand the difference between needs and wants. You'll soon realize you already have everything you need, and most of what you want.

CHAPTER 7
CLEVER KIDS' MEALS

Luckily for the Frugal Foodie, kids are pretty cheap dates. Their personal food pyramid is built on a solid foundation of "white" food: rice, pasta, bread, cheese, apples, and bananas. The clever cook can create meals that kids will eat and that will give them the fuel they need to plow through their active days. When you start to fret that Junior isn't getting enough variety of foods (or even colors of foods) in her diet, remember what a wise mom who was raising teenagers and a preschooler told me, "Trust me, they grow up big and strong no matter what they eat!"

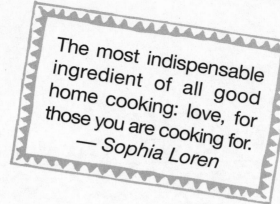

The most indispensable ingredient of all good home cooking: love, for those you are cooking for.
— Sophia Loren

THE USUAL SUSPECTS

I've heard all about those mythic French kids who sit politely at the table and say, "Maman, je veux plus d'escargots."* But *bonne chance* to the American mom who tries to get her kids to eat more than applesauce, chicken nuggets, and mac and cheese.

As long as the foods that make up your kids' diet can be counted on one hand, you might as well make those items as wholesome and inexpensive as possible.

[*"Mom, can I have some more snails, please?"]

Mrs. Spector's Applesauce

My grandma was a classic cook of the 50s. She embraced every can, box, prefab mix, and corporate food-preserving process as a gift from science to her kitchen.

But twice a year, for Passover and Hanukkah, she hauled out her heavy pressure cooker and made up a batch of homemade sweet-tart applesauce. I still smuggle a jar of it in my luggage after a trip home for the holidays.

Not only was Grandma's applesauce homemade, it usually featured the decidedly old-fashioned vegetable rhubarb. If you can find fresh rhubarb, add some in 1-inch chunks to the apples before you cook the sauce. It imparts a beautiful rosy color and puckery tartness.

1/4 cup granulated sugar

1/4 cup brown sugar

4 strips of lemon peel

My own appreciation for creative, good food has been enhanced by sharing it on a regular basis with three-, four-, and five-year-olds.
— Mollie Katzen

juice of 1 lemon

1 teaspoon ground cinnamon

1/2 cup water

4 pounds tart green apples, cored, peeled, and chopped into 1-inch pieces

In a large saucepan over medium heat, combine the sugars, lemon peel, juice, cinnamon, and water, and stir to dissolve the sugars. Add the apples and cover the pot. Simmer until fall-apart tender, about 15–20 minutes.

You've got a few options for saucing the apples. If you have a food mill, use it. Or you can press the apples through a fine sieve, or mash them with a potato masher.

Makes 4–5 cups.

Better Chicken Nuggets

These crispy bites are a bit of a production, but they freeze well and you can make a lot at once. Get the kids involved with the dipping and breading. Yeah, they'll make a mess, but its good, clean fun.

A quick bath in seasoned yogurt keeps the chicken moist and flavorful. The flour, breadcrumbs, cornmeal, and panko combine to give the nuggets a crunch and color that rival the fast-food versions, and cooking on a rack helps the nuggets crisp on all sides.

6 ounces plain yogurt

1 clove garlic, minced

2 boneless, skinless chicken breasts, cut into 3-inch pieces

⅓ cup flour

⅓ cup cornmeal

3 eggs, beaten

1/2 cup panko (Japanese breadcrumbs)

1/2 cup fine breadcrumbs

1 tablespoon vegetable oil

salt and pepper, to taste

Mix the yogurt and garlic in a medium bowl. Season with salt and pepper. Add the chicken pieces and toss to coat. Cover and marinate for an hour.

Preheat oven to 450°F.

Place a wire rack on a cookie sheet or rimmed baking sheet.

Set out three shallow bowls or pie plates. In the first, place the flour, cornmeal, salt, and pepper and mix well. In the second, place the eggs and beat well with a fork. In the third, place the panko and fine breadcrumbs and mix with the vegetable oil.

Remove the chicken pieces from the marinade, scraping off as much of it as possible with your fingers. Dip the chicken pieces in the flour and cornmeal mixture and shake off the excess. Then dip 'em in the eggs and give 'em another shake. Finally, press them into the crumbs to coat completely.

Place the chicken pieces on the rack in a single layer. Spray the tops with vegetable oil spray. Bake for 7–8 minutes, turn the pieces over, and bake for an additional 7–8 minutes, until golden brown.

Makes approximately 24 nuggets.

My Kid's Mom's Mac and Cheese

My mom's mac came from a small blue box and the "cheese" was a reconstituted powder. A friend of mine in college called the stuff "Macaroni and Yellow."

This Mac and Cheese was inspired by my friend Jenny's family recipe. The first time I had it I was amazed. It tasted like . . . like . . . cheese!

While my own position on cheese is the sharper the better, I've found that kids prefer a milder sauce. Experiment with different types of cheese to suit your family's taste.

1 cup grated mild Cheddar cheese
1 cup grated Monterey Jack cheese
3/4 cup warm milk
1 tablespoon flour
2 tablespoons melted butter
1 garlic clove, crushed
1/2 pound large elbow macaroni, cooked
salt and pepper, to taste

Preheat oven to 325°F. Butter a casserole dish.

Blend cheeses, milk, flour, butter, and garlic in a blender or food processor. In a bowl, mix the sauce with the macaroni to coat completely. Turn the mixture into the prepared dish and bake for 45 minutes.

Makes 6 servings.

HIPPIE FOOD

Growing up in the 1970s, I experienced all of the well-meaning fads of the era: carob, sprout sandwiches, and dry and suspiciously crunchy homemade wheat breads.

While I'm glad to see many of these culinary experiments go the way of granny glasses and dashikis, some hippy food is worth resurrecting.

Crunchy Granola

Homemade granola smells wonderful while it's baking, and it is much healthier than commercial brands, which are loaded with hidden oils and sugars. Have fun playing with different types of fruits, nuts, and spices (see guide below).

4 cups old-fashioned rolled oats

1 cup nuts, toasted and chopped

1/4 cup packed light brown sugar

1/2 teaspoon ground cinnamon

1/4 teaspoon salt

1/2 cup butter

1/4 cup honey

1 teaspoon vanilla extract

1 cup chopped dried fruit

Preheat oven to 300°F.

Line a rimmed baking sheet with foil and grease generously with vegetable oil or spray.

Mix the oats, nuts, sugar, cinnamon, and salt in a large bowl. In a small saucepan over low heat, melt the butter and honey, stirring to combine. Add the vanilla and stir.

Pour the honey butter over the oat mixture and stir to combine. Turn the mixture onto the prepared pan and spread in an even layer. Bake for 15 minutes, remove from the oven, and stir. Return the granola to the oven and bake for 10–15 minutes more, checking to make sure it doesn't burn.

Cool in the pan on a cooling rack, then transfer to an airtight container and stir in the dried fruit.

Makes approximately 6 cups.

DRIED FRUIT	NUT	OPTIONS
banana chips	peanuts	Add 1/4 cup wheat germ to the oats.
cherries	almonds	Add 1 teaspoon almond extract with the vanilla.
apple	walnuts	Replace the honey with maple syrup.
mango	pecans	Replace the cinnamon with ground ginger.
raisins	sunflower seeds	Add 1/2 cup unsweetened coconut to the oats.

Lentil Burgers

This burger is cheap and easy, and tasty — and using red lentils gives it an attractive color more similar to beef than other veggie burgers. A great recipe to have on hand for meatless dinners and as an alternative for vegetarian guests at your BBQ.

1 tablespoon olive oil

1/2 small onion, peeled and finely chopped

1 clove garlic, minced

1 carrot, scrubbed and finely grated

1/2 cup dry red lentils

2 cups water

1 egg, beaten

1/2 cup breadcrumbs

salt and pepper, to taste

In a large lidded skillet, heat the olive oil over medium heat. Add the onion and cook for 5 minutes. Add the garlic and carrot and cook for 2–3 minutes. Stir in the lentils and water and bring to a boil. Reduce heat to low, cover, and simmer for 20 minutes, until the liquid is cooked away. Cool the lentils for 10–15 minutes.

Preheat the oven to 350°F and oil or spray

a cookie sheet.

When the lentil mixture has cooled, add the egg and breadcrumbs. Mix with your hands. Add more breadcrumbs if the mixture doesn't hold together. Season with salt and pepper.

Form the mixture into 4 patties and place them on the baking sheet. Bake for 10–15 minutes, until firm.

Serve on hamburger buns with ketchup, lettuce, and tomato.

Makes 4 burgers.

Share the Love Breakfast Bread

This takes some time to get started, but it is worth the wait. Keep it going and you'll never need to buy yeast for it again.

FRIENDSHIP BREAD STARTER

1/4 ounce active dry yeast (1 packet)

1/4 cup warm water

3 cups all-purpose flour

3 cups sugar

3 cups whole milk

Day 1: In a large nonmetal bowl, dissolve yeast in warm water. With a wooden spoon, stir in 1 cup flour, 1 cup sugar, and 1 cup milk. Cover loosely and leave out at room temperature.

Day 2: Stir starter once.

Day 3: Stir starter once.

Day 4: Stir starter once.

Day 5: Stir in 1 cup flour, 1 cup sugar, and 1 cup milk.

Day 6: Stir starter once.

Day 7: Stir starter once.

Day 8: Stir starter once.

Day 9: stir Starter once.

Day 10: Stir in 1 cup flour, 1 cup sugar, and 1 cup milk.

Use 1 cup of this starter mixture to make one batch of Friendship Bread. Divide the remaining starter between two 1-gallon ziplock bags and give them to two friends, along with a copy of the recipe for finishing the starter and baking the bread.

TO FINISH THE STARTER

1 cup Friendship Bread Starter

2 1/2 cups all-purpose flour, divided

2 1/2 cups sugar, divided

2 1/2 cups whole milk, divided

5 1-gallon-size ziplock freezer bags

Day 1: Transfer starter to a ziplock bag, seal the bag, and leave it out at room temperature.

Day 2: Squish the bag, letting air out as needed.

Day 3: Squish the bag, letting air out as needed.

Day 4: Squish the bag, letting air out as needed.

Day 5: Squish the bag, letting air out as needed.

Day 6: Add 1 cup flour, 1 cup sugar, and 1 cup milk. Squish the bag and leave it out at room temperature.

Day 7: Squish the bag, letting air out as needed.

Day 8: Squish the bag, letting air out as needed.

Day 9: Squish the bag, letting air out as needed.

Day 10: Empty the bag into a large non-metal bowl and add remaining 1 1/2 cups each flour, sugar, and milk. Mix well. Put one cup of starter into each of four ziplock freezer bags, sealing out the air. Date the bags and give three of them to friends with a copy of the recipe for how to bake the bread. Save the fourth one for yourself as the starter for the next batch. (Freeze it until you're ready to make the next batch. Allow it to return to room temperature before use.) You will use the remaining starter in the bowl to bake 2 loaves of bread (recipe follows).

TO BAKE THE BREAD

1 tablespoon butter, softened, for greasing loaf pans

3 eggs, beaten

1 cup vegetable oil

2 teaspoons vanilla extract

1/2 cup milk

1 1/4 cups sugar, divided

3 teaspoons ground cinnamon, divided

1/2 teaspoon baking powder

1/2 teaspoon baking soda

1/2 teaspoon salt

2 1/4 cups all-purpose flour

Preheat oven to 325°F. Butter two 9-inch x 5-inch loaf pans and set aside.

To the remaining starter in the bowl add the eggs, oil, vanilla, milk, 1 cup sugar, 2 teaspoons cinnamon, baking powder, baking soda, salt, and flour. Mix well. Pour the batter into the prepared loaf pans.

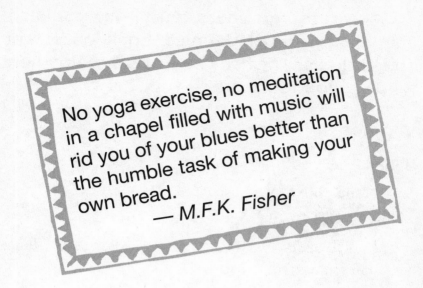

No yoga exercise, no meditation in a chapel filled with music will rid you of your blues better than the humble task of making your own bread.
— M.F.K. Fisher

Combine remaining 1 teaspoon cinnamon and remaining 1/4 cup sugar, and sprinkle it over the batter. Bake for one hour, then cool on a rack.

Makes 2 loaves.

BABY FOOD

I know, I know, you're thinking the last thing a new mom has time for is making baby food, for goodness sakes. But the truth is, making baby food is some of the easiest and most cost-effective cooking you can do. And because the little bundles of joy don't eat much, you can make a month's worth of food in just a couple of hours.

Make sure you check with your pediatrician or consult a detailed book on infant and child care before you introduce any new foods or food formats to your baby.

Veggies

BOILABLE

carrots, scrubbed and thinly sliced

sweet potatoes, peeled and diced

green beans, washed, ends snipped, and cut into small pieces

split peas, picked over and rinsed

Boil prepared veggies in water until fall-apart tender; depending on the food, for 10 minutes (carrots) to 40 minutes (split peas).

If you're making a lot of food to store, work in batches. Remove the cooked veggies from the pot with a slotted spoon and keep the water boiling, then add the next veg and start round two.

Reserve some of the cooking liquid, then strain the veggies. Transfer to a food processor or blender and whirl into a puree. Add a bit of the cooking liquid if it's too thick.

BAKEABLE

squash (acorn, winter, or butternut)

Cut squashes in half and scoop out the seeds. Place them, cut side down, on a baking pan lined with foil, and bake at 350°F for 40–45 minutes. Cool completely and scoop out the flesh. Puree in a blender or food processor, adding a little water, if needed.

Fruits

STEAMABLE

peaches, peeled, stoned, and sliced

plums, peeled, stoned, and sliced

apricots, peeled, stoned, and sliced

apples, peeled, cored, and sliced

pears, peeled, cored, and sliced

Set a steamer basket over an inch or two of boiling water. Add the fruit and steam until fall-apart tender, about 3–5 minutes. Reserve some of the cooking liquid, then strain the fruit. Transfer to a food processor or blender and whirl into a puree. Add a bit of the cooking liquid if it's too thick. If it's too thin, add a bit of cooked rice and puree until smooth.

MASH AND GO

avocados

bananas

Cereal

whole oats

barley

brown rice

Grind ⅓ cup of oats, barley, and/or rice into a very fine powder in a food processor. A clean coffee grinder also works well.

Bring 1 cup of water to a boil. Gradually add the powdered grains, stirring constantly. Simmer for 10 minutes. Cool and serve.

FRUGAL FOODIE TIP:
ICE, ICE, BABY

The easiest way to store homemade baby food is to freeze it in ice cube trays. Wash an ice cube tray very well with hot soapy water or run it through the dishwasher. Fill the tray with purees. Each cube is about one fluid ounce of food. Baby food can be kept frozen for up to 3 months.

Meats

1 cup cooked lean, boneless beef, chicken, white fish, or turkey

1/4 cup water or reserved vegetable cooking liquid

Bake the meat in a 350°F oven until thoroughly cooked. Use a meat thermometer, just to be on the safe side. Beef should be cooked to 150–160°F, chicken or turkey to 165–175°F, fish to 145–150°F.

Puree the cooked meat in a food processor until very fine. Slowly add the water until it forms a paste.

FINGER FOODS

At about 6 months, babies are ready to feed themselves using their own fingers. Make it even easier for them by making the foods finger-shaped!

Cookie fingers

1/4 cup butter

1 tablespoon brown sugar

1/4 cup milk

3/4 cup flour

1/4 cup wheat germ

Preheat oven to 350°F.

Grease a cookie sheet.

Beat the butter and sugar until fluffy. Gradually add the milk and blend well. Add the flour and wheat germ and mix until a dough forms. Turn the dough onto a floured work surface and knead until smooth.

Divide the dough into 12 pieces. Roll each piece into a little log, place the logs on the prepared cookie sheet, and flatten them into fingers.

Bake for 30–35 minutes, until golden and hardened. Cool completely on a cooling rack.

Makes 1 dozen biscuits.

Chicken fingers

1 medium carrot, scrubbed and cut into 1-inch pieces

1/2 small apple, peeled, cored, and cut into 1-inch pieces

1 small potato, peeled and boiled until tender

1/2 garlic clove

1 tablespoon onion, minced

1/2 pound skinless and boneless chicken, dark or white meat, cut into 2- to 3-inch pieces

1 small egg yolk, beaten

2 tablespoons fresh breadcrumbs

Preheat oven to 350°F.

Line a cookie sheet with foil.

Place the carrot, apple, potato, garlic, and onion in the bowl of a food processor and pulse until very finely chopped. Remove the veggies to a medium bowl. Put the chicken in the food processor and pulse until very finely ground. Add the chicken, egg yolk, and breadcrumbs to the veggies and mix with your hands until well combined. Roll the mixture by tablespoons into little sausages and place them on the prepared baking sheet.

Bake for 15 minutes, until browned and firm.

Makes about 20 fingers.

Veggie fingers

1/2 pound broccoli florets

1/4 cup breadcrumbs

3/4 cup mild Cheddar cheese, shredded

2 tablespoons milk

2 tablespoons vegetable oil

1 1/2 teaspoons baking powder

2 tablespoons flour

Preheat oven to 375°F.

Grease a cookie sheet.

Boil or steam the broccoli until it's falling-apart tender. Chop very fine and place in a medium bowl. Add the rest of the ingredients and mix until you can form it into shapes with your hands, adding a little more flour if too thin, or water if too firm. Form the mixture into little logs and flatten on the prepared cookie

FRUGAL FOODIE TIP: COOCHIE COUSCOUS

Couscous is a cheap, easy, and healthy addition to pureed fruits and veggies when your baby is ready for more texture. Simply boil 1 cup of water, remove from heat, add 1/2 cup of couscous, and stir. Cover the pot and let the couscous steep for 5 minutes. Fluff with a fork and add a bit to your fruit or veggie puree.

sheet. Bake for 20–25 minutes. Cool slightly, and serve warm.

Makes about 15 fingers.

COLORFUL BIRTHDAY PARTY

It's amazing what a little food coloring will do. Everyday foods become party-special with a drop or two of your kids' favorite food coloring.

Concerns about the health effects of food coloring have been largely put to rest. Red M&Ms have been back in the bag for years, and a few drops of coloring in birthday party and holiday treats will have no negative health effects.

These ideas for food and activities are bursting with beautiful colors, and will make an easy, festive, and inexpensive birthday celebration for a young child.

Kaleidoscope Popcorn

Make several batches in several flavors and serve in big, clear bowls — you'll have a bright and beautiful centerpiece for the table. You'll also probably have lots of leftovers, which can be sent home with the kiddies in clear plastic bags tied with a ribbon as party favors.

1/4 cup butter

3/4 cup sugar

1 package fruit-flavored Jello (3-ounce size)

3 tablespoons light corn syrup

3 tablespoons water

1/4 teaspoon baking soda

8 cups popped popcorn (about 1/2 cup of kernels)

Preheat oven to 300°F.

Line two rimmed baking sheets with foil and grease with cooking oil spray.

Melt the butter in a heavy-bottomed saucepan. Add sugar, Jello, corn syrup, and water. Cook over medium heat, stirring often, until the mixture boils. Simmer for 5 minutes. Add baking soda, stirring well to combine.

In a large bowl, pour Jello mixture evenly over the popcorn and mix well to coat evenly. Spread the coated popcorn on the prepared baking sheets and bake for 10 minutes. Stir it and bake for an additional 5 minutes. The popcorn should be dry and crisp. Bake longer if needed, but check every 2 minutes or so to be sure it doesn't burn.

Slide the foil onto cooling racks and cool the popcorn completely. Break into small clusters.

Makes 8 cups.

Purple Milk from the Purple Cow

When I was in preschool, my friend Adam's parents were the ultimate health food nuts.

A full wall of their pantry was lined with hundreds of jars of beans, lentils, powders, and spices, and everything their children ate was homemade or organic. Lunches and dinners at their house were sketchy bets, and I was always told, "If you're looking for dessert — you came to the wrong house."

But they did offer as an everyday treat "purple milk from the purple cow." I now know this was simply (organic, hormone-free) milk with a drop or two of food coloring added (probably extracted from organic beets), but at the time I was sure that somewhere there was indeed a purple cow that gave this pretty milk — and I even believed it tasted like "purple."

1 quart milk

12 drops red food coloring

8 drops blue food coloring

Pour milk into a clear pitcher. Add food coloring and stir to blend. Serve in clear cups or glasses.

Makes 4 1-cup servings.

Peanut Butter Picassos

Gather the kids to a newspaper-lined table and let them paint the bread for their sandwiches.

milk

food coloring

white bread

peanut butter and jelly

Fill each cavity of an ice cube tray or muffin tin half full with milk. Place a few drops of food coloring in each section to make bright colors. Let the kids "paint" two pieces of bread with the colored milk using new, clean paint brushes. Toast the bread slightly to dry the "paint," and use the bread for making PB&Js (or cheese, or tuna, or whatever sandwiches you can get them to eat).

Please Eat the Play Dough

Edible play dough does double duty as a party activity and take-home favor.

SUPER SWEET

1 cup butter

1 cup light corn syrup

1 1/4 cups powdered sugar

1 1/4 cups powdered milk

In an electric mixer, beat the butter and corn syrup until well blended. Gradually add the sugar and powdered milk, until a stiff dough forms.

Turn the dough out onto a board dusted with powdered sugar, and knead it a few times. Divide the dough into 4 pieces.

Take one of the pieces and press your thumb into it, making a cavity, then drip a few drops of food coloring into the cavity. Pinch it closed, and knead the dough until you have a uniform color. Repeat with the remaining pieces.

Makes 4 cups.

NOT SO SWEET

2 8-ounce packages of cream cheese

1 cup nonfat dry milk

2 tablespoons honey

In an electric mixer, cream the cream cheese and honey until fluffy. Gradually add the powdered milk, until a stiff dough forms.

Turn the dough out on a board dusted with flour, and knead a few times. Divide the dough into 4 pieces.

Take one of the pieces and press your thumb into it, making a cavity, then drip a few drops of food coloring into the cavity. Pinch it closed, and knead the dough until you have a uniform color. Repeat with the remaining pieces.

Makes about 2 1/2 cups.

Edible Finger Paints

Cover your table well with newspaper before you start this delightfully messy activity, or set up the paints and paper outside.

sweetened condensed milk, vanilla pudding, or light corn syrup

food coloring

Fill each cavity of an ice cube tray or muffin tin half full with condensed milk, pudding, or corn syrup. Place a few drops of food coloring in each section to make bright, happy colors. Let the kids dig in and color on paper, sheets of foil, or coloring pages.

Paint with Pasta

Making pasta mosaics is much more fun when the noodles are dyed vibrant colors.

2 cups rice or pasta in small, interesting shapes

ziplock bags

food coloring

white glue

paper, picture frames, or lidded boxes

Pour 1 teaspoon of water and 10 drops of food coloring into the corner of a ziplock bag. Add 1/2 cup rice or pasta to the bag, zip it closed, then mush it around until well saturated with the dye.

Spread on a wax-paper-lined baking sheet and let dry for about an hour.

Brush a piece of paper, picture frame, or small cardboard box with white glue and let the kids "paint" pictures or designs with the colored pasta.

Makes 2 cups.

You don't have to cook fancy or complicated masterpieces — just good food from fresh ingredients.
— Julia Child

ORGANIC PANIC!

Organic or not? It can be a tough choice for the Frugal Foodie. You know that organics are more sustainable, healthier, and tastier — but, oh, the sticker shock!

The good news is that it's not an all-or-nothing game. The Environmental Working Group has developed a "Dirty Dozen" list of the 12 fruits and veggies that have been found to have the highest concentration of pesticides, and another list of the produce that has the lowest amount of pesticide. Make the effort to choose organic when buying foods from the "dirty" list — particularly if you are serving to young children — and save your coin and buy grocery-store produce for the items on the "clean" list.

The Dirty Dozen

apples	peaches
celery	pears
cherries	potatoes
imported grapes	spinach
lettuce	strawberries
nectarines	sweet bell peppers

The Clean Team

asparagus	frozen sweet corn
avocados	kiwi fruit
bananas	mangoes
broccoli	onions
cabbage	papayas
frozen peas	pineapples

CENTS-ABLE SOLUTIONS: SNACKS FOR STARVING STUDENTS

Packaged snacks are expensive, or full of chemicals, or both. Successful snacking means having an arsenal of staples in your pantry and freezer, and adding a few home-made treats to the mix. You and your kids can whip up tasty, filling, and wholesome after-school snacks in a jiffy. Here's a full month's worth of after-school yummies that can be eaten at home or in transit.

- Bagel and cream cheese
- Cinnamon toast
- Apple fries with "ketchup": Peel and core an apple and cut it into thick sticks. Mix a little yogurt with seed-less strawberry jam to make "ketchup." To take this snack to go, put a little of the dip in the bottom of a container (recycled yogurt cups work great) and add the apple fries.

251

- Tortilla roll-up with sliced turkey and cheese
- Cereal: At home, in a bowl with milk, or on the go, in a ziplock bag
- Popcorn
- Bananarito: Spread a tortilla with peanut butter, add half a banana, and roll up.
- Celery filled with peanut butter and dotted with raisins
- Graham crackers with cream cheese or peanut butter
- Corn muffins
- Toasted banana bread
- Yogurt smoothie: Blend yogurt, fruit, and milk until smooth. Keep fruit that is a little bruised or just past its prime in the freezer, and pop it in a smoothie.
- Plain ice cream cone filled with tuna or egg salad
- Minipizza: Top an English muffin, bagel, pita, or other sturdy bread with marinara sauce and cheese, and toast for 10 minutes. You can even use ketchup in a pinch.
- Waffles: Bake a few extra on the

weekend, and freeze. They can be toasted and topped with peanut butter or applesauce.

- Breakfast burrito: Scrambled eggs and cheese wrapped in a tortilla
- Yogurt Jello cups: Combine 2 cups boiling water and a large package of Jello. Add fruit according to the package directions plus one 6-ounce tub of fruit-flavored yogurt. Chill in recycled yogurt cups.
- Munchie mix: Mix 4 or 5 of your kids' favorite dried or crunchy things: pretzels, banana chips, oyster crackers, Goldfish™ crackers, raisins, yogurt chips, cereal.
- Banana dog: Spread one half of a hot dog bun with peanut butter, add a whole peeled banana, and slather with jelly.
- No-bake kitchen sink bars: Mix 1/2 cup peanut butter and 1/3 cup honey in a large bowl, and microwave for 30 seconds. Add 3 cups of your favorite granolas and cereals and 1 cup of chocolate chips, raisins, dried fruit, or fruit chips, in

any combination. Mix well, spread in a greased 8-inch square pan, and chill until firm. Cut into bars, and serve.

CHAPTER 8
MIDNIGHT SNACKS

I did a survey of my friends to see to what lengths they had gone to satisfy late-night hunger pangs when there was "nothing" in the house. The results were both eye-opening and stomach-turning:

Chunks of frozen pumpkin bread chiseled from a loaf

Apple butter and caramel sauce

Saltines with mayo and onions

Spoonful of peanut butter dipped in a bag of chocolate chips

Crushed Coco Puffs with chocolate syrup and Reddi-wip®

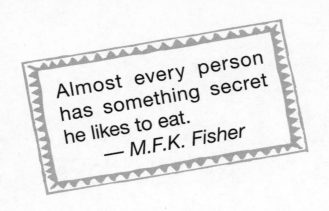

Almost every person has something secret he likes to eat.
— M.F.K. Fisher

Ritz crackers with BBQ sauce

Spoonful of Crisco dipped in sugar

I knew I had reached my personal rock bottom when I filled an ice cream cone with marshmallows and chocolate chips, microwaved it for 15 seconds, and ate my ersatz s'more washed down with orange juice.

The goal of this chapter is to save you, dear reader, from a similar fate. Spend a few minutes preparing and planning for your midnight minifeast and you'll not only have a yummy treat — you'll respect yourself in the morning.

MEDITERRANEAN MEZE MUNCHIES

The Meds have it all figured out. Not only is their diet among the world's healthiest and most delicious, but they've raised snacking to an art form. Like Spanish tapas and Chinese dim sum, Mediterranean *meze* are yummy little bits and bites of savory goodness that can be eaten as snacks or combined to make a meal.

Keep a pack of pita bread in the freezer — it comes back to life in just a few minutes in a toaster oven and is the perfect delivery device for dips. Don't worry about overtoasting — it's equally good as a crispy cracker or as soft bread.

Aubergenius Dip

2 whole garlic cloves, unpeeled

1/4 cup olive oil

1 large eggplant

2 tablespoons lemon juice

1/4 cup finely chopped parsley

3 tablespoons tahini (optional)

salt, to taste

Preheat oven to 450°F.

Place the garlic cloves on a small square of aluminum foil and drizzle with a little of the olive oil. Close up the foil and seal around the garlic cloves.

Place the whole eggplant on a baking sheet and prick with a fork several times. Roast in the oven for about 35 minutes — it should be very tender. After 15 minutes of cooking, toss the garlic packet onto the baking sheet.

Remove the baking sheet from the oven. Using two forks, immediately tear the eggplant open and scrape the pulp right onto the hot baking sheet. This will help evaporate some of the liquid. Discard the skin and transfer the eggplant to a bowl. Open the garlic packet and squeeze the soft garlic cloves onto the eggplant. Continue to shred the eggplant until it's a spreadable consistency. Add the remaining ingredients and stir to combine.

Makes about 2 cups.

Kale Krisps

1 head Tuscan or dino kale, washed and cut into tortilla-chip-sized pieces

1/2 tablespoon balsamic vinegar

2 tablespoons olive oil

salt and pepper

Preheat oven to 300°F.

Place the kale pieces in a bowl and drizzle with vinegar and olive oil. Turn the leaves a couple of times to coat. Sprinkle with salt and pepper. Arrange leaves in single layer on 2 large baking sheets. Bake until crisp, about 30–35 minutes, tossing halfway through cooking time and turning the heat down if they get brown before they get crisp.

Transfer to a rack to cool.

Makes about 6 cups.

Marinated Olives

2 cups good-quality green or black olives

6 sprigs of fresh rosemary

6 strips of lemon or orange peel

2/3 cup olive oil

3 garlic cloves

1/2 teaspoon salt

1/4 teaspoon red pepper flakes

1 bay leaf

Cut a small slit in each olive with a sharp paring knife. Put the olives in a 1-pint

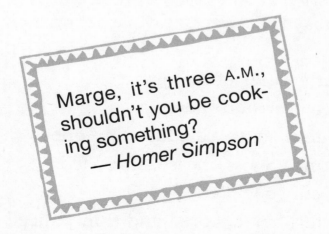

Marge, it's three A.M., shouldn't you be cooking something?
— Homer Simpson

glass jar. Add the rest of the ingredients, seal the jar tightly, and invert several times to blend the flavors. Store in the refrigerator for at least a week to give the olives time to soak up the yumminess.

Makes 2 cups.

HOT, TOASTY, CHEESY, AND MELTY

A grilled cheese sandwich is an ideal midnight snack. It requires few ingredients, cooks quickly, and is a good base for variations using what you have on hand.

Both bread and shredded hard cheeses can be kept in the freezer — ready to be married and melted when the mood strikes.

Ted's Grilled Cheese Sandwich

My friend Maria's husband, Ted, contributed a version of this sandwich to the book *Food Men Love* (Conari Press, 2001). I love the play of sweet, savory, crunchy, and gooey.

2 large rings of red onion

1/2 tablespoon sherry

1 ounce sharp Cheddar, shredded

1 ounce Swiss cheese, shredded

1/2 ounce feta cheese

1/4 tart apple, cored and thinly sliced

2 slices honey-nut wheat bread, buttered on one side

Dijon mustard

In a small skillet over medium heat, sauté the onion rings in the sherry for 3–4 minutes. Set aside.

On the unbuttered side of one slice of bread, layer the cheeses, apple slices, and onion rings, beginning and ending with cheese. Spread the unbuttered side of the other slice of bread with the mustard and top the sandwich, buttered side up. Zap the sandwich in the microwave for 20 seconds to give the cheese a head start.

Toast the sandwich in the skillet over medium heat for about 3 minutes on each side.

Makes 1 sandwich.

Provençal Quesadilla

This delicious snack was invented when there was "nothing" in the fridge.

1 clove garlic, minced

olive oil

2 flour tortillas

1 tablespoon goat cheese

1 tablespoon cream cheese

1/4 cup cooked leftover chicken, finely chopped

1/4 teaspoon fresh rosemary

In a skillet, sauté the garlic over medium heat in a little olive oil for 2–3 minutes. Remove the garlic, reserving the skillet.

Spread each tortilla with half of the cream cheese and half of the goat cheese, mashing them together right on the tortilla. Sprinkle the chicken, rosemary, and garlic on one tortilla, and top with the other, cheese side down.

Reheat the skillet over medium-high heat. Film the hot skillet with olive oil. Place the quesadilla in the pan and cook until crisp and golden, about 5–6 minutes. Flip and cook the other side.

Cool for 3–4 minutes and slice into 8 wedges.

Serves 1.

Croque-Monsieur et Madame

I wanted to know what Julia Child had to say on the subject of the classic French grilled cheese and ham, the croque-monsieur. Not surprisingly, on one of her cooking shows, the unfussy Ms. Child eschewed the time-consuming additions of mornay or béchamel sauce that you see in some older recipes and focused on the basics: cheese, ham, and bread.

Clarifying butter is a crucial step. The butter gives a rich taste to the sandwich, and when the solids are removed it can hold up to a higher heat without scorching.

2 slices home-style white bread

1 tablespoon mayonnaise (see page 93 for a homemade mayo recipe)

Dijon mustard

2 large slices Swiss cheese, enough for two layers totally covering the bread

1 slice ham, fat removed, and trimmed to fit the bread

2 tablespoons clarified butter (method follows)

Preheat oven to 300°F.

Place the two slices of bread next to each other on a cutting board. Spread an even coating of mayonnaise on each, and then a bit of mustard. Lay a slice of cheese on one piece of bread, followed by the ham, then the remaining slice of cheese. Invert the other piece of bread onto the sandwich, mayonnaise side down, and press firmly. Rotate and press several times to hold the sandwich together.

Film an ovenproof skillet with a tablespoon of clarified butter and set over medium-high heat. When the butter is very hot but not browning, lower the heat to medium and lay the sandwich in the skillet, pressing down several times. Cook for 2 minutes.

Lift the sandwich from the skillet with a spatula and add another tablespoon of clarified butter to the pan. Return the sandwich to the skillet and brown on the other side, pressing down several times.

Place the skillet in the oven and bake for 5–6 minutes, until the cheese is fully melted.

Makes 1 sandwich.

Clarified Butter

1 stick butter

Melt butter in a clear glass 2-cup measuring cup in the microwave at full power for 1 minute. Continue to zap it in 30-second intervals until completely melted. The top will be covered in a layer of foam. Under the foam is the butterfat you're after, and under that is the water and solids you want to discard.

First, skim the foam off the top with a

spoon. Then carefully spoon out the butterfat, leaving the milky solids in the measuring cup. Or, after skimming off the foam, slowly pour the liquid into a second clear measuring cup, leaving the milky solids.

Store clarified butter in glass jar in the fridge for up to 3 months, or in the freezer for up to a year.

Makes approximately 3/4 cup.

Tranny Sammie

Turn your croque-monsieur into a croque-madame in one easy operation!

1 croque-monsieur

1/2 tablespoon clarified butter

1 egg

salt

Remove the sandwich from the skillet to a cutting board while you prepare the egg.

Heat clarified butter in the skillet over medium-high heat. Carefully crack the egg in the center of the skillet, making sure not to break the yolk. Sprinkle a little salt on the egg, and add a teaspoon of water to the pan. Cover and cook for

3–4 minutes. Slide the egg onto the top of the sandwich.

SECRET SWEETS

I try to keep packaged cookies and ice cream out of the house (I don't need the hit to my wallet or dress size), but I do have a decidedly sweet tooth that practically throbs a couple of hours after dinner.

These single-serving treats are easy to stash in the freezer or whip up in a jiff when you're looking for a late-night shot o' sugar.

Ice Cream Sandwiches

1 cup flour

1/2 cup cocoa powder

1/4 teaspoon salt

1/8 teaspoon baking soda

2 large eggs

2/3 cup sugar

1/4 cup chocolate syrup (recipe follows)

8 tablespoons unsalted butter, melted

2 pints of your favorite flavor of ice cream

Preheat oven to 350°F.

Spray a rimmed baking sheet with cooking oil spray and line with foil or parchment.

Mix flour, cocoa powder, salt, and baking soda in a medium bowl. In a large bowl, beat eggs, sugar, and chocolate syrup. Add melted butter and whisk until fully incorporated.

Add the dry ingredients to the wet ones. With a rubber spatula, fold the batter until fully incorporated. Pour batter into prepared baking sheet, spreading evenly. Bake for 10 to 12 minutes. Cool in the pan on a wire rack for 5 minutes, then run a paring knife around the perimeter of the baking sheet to loosen. Turn the cookie onto a work surface or large cutting board and peel off the parchment. Cool for 30 minutes. Cut the cookie in half crosswise.

Meanwhile, soften the ice cream in the refrigerator for 15 minutes. Transfer to an electric mixer and beat for 2–3 minutes. Working quickly, spread the ice cream on half of the cookie. Top with the other half. Put the cookie sheet in the freezer and freeze for an hour.

Remove from the freezer and cut into 8 pieces. Wrap each sandwich individually in plastic wrap or waxed paper and freeze for up to 4 weeks.

Makes 8 sandwiches.

Chocolate Syrup

2 tablespoons cocoa powder

1/4 cup water

1/2 cup sugar

pinch of salt

dash of vanilla extract

Mix cocoa powder, water, and sugar in a small saucepan. Bring to a boil, stirring constantly. Boil for 3 minutes. Remove from heat and stir in salt and vanilla.

You'll use 1/4 cup of syrup in the cookies for the ice cream sandwiches. The leftover syrup makes exquisite chocolate milk or hot chocolate.

(adapted liberally from *Cook's Illustrated*)

Coffee Mug Cake

No one's going to accuse this cake of being gourmet, but when you're desperate for something warm, sweet, and chocolaty, this will do the trick — and it's much tastier and cheaper than the microwaveable single-serve cakes that have begun hitting the store shelves.

1/4 cup flour

1/4 cup sugar

3 tablespoons cocoa powder

pinch of salt

1 egg

1/4 cup milk

3 tablespoons vegetable oil

1/4 teaspoon vanilla extract

In a very large coffee mug (or small ovenproof ceramic bowl), mix the flour, sugar, cocoa powder, and salt with a fork. Add the egg, milk, oil, and vanilla and mix with the fork until well blended.

If you're desperate, you can cook this in the microwave for 3 minutes at full power. Let it cool for 1–2 minutes before digging in. The texture is a little . . . well, spongy, but the cake is warm, gooey, and chocolaty, and you could do a lot worse at midnight. The experience is vastly improved with a scoop of vanilla ice cream.

If you can hold on for a bit, bake the cake in a 350°F toaster oven (or regular oven) for 30–40 minutes. The cake texture will be much better, and you'll have a lavalike center of hot chocolaty goodness.

Serves one.

CCC's on the QT

Keep a freezer bag or other container of chocolate chip cookie dough balls on hand, and you're less than 20 minutes away from fresh, hot cookies. And if you're really impatient, you can nibble on the dough balls straight from the freezer. Hey, it's midnight — no one will see you.

I developed this recipe with a lot of research, trial and error, and advice from experts. My friend Beth's delectable cookies result from a little extra salt, and Maria's sister-in-law swears the secret is doubling the vanilla. Mrs. Field adds texture and depth with ground oatmeal, and for Pam Anderson (the *USA Today* editor, not the *Baywatch* babe) its all about technique: freeze first, bake later.

2 cups all-purpose flour

1 cup oatmeal, ground fine in a food processor

[handwritten: 2 cups oatmeal]

1 teaspoon baking powder

[handwritten: 1 cup WFm on degree]

1/2 teaspoon baking soda

[handwritten: Wheat Flour Pre BP]

1 1/2 teaspoons salt

1 cup (2 sticks) butter, softened

[handwritten: Flour Brown sugar milk]

3/4 cup granulated sugar

3/4 cup packed brown sugar

2 large eggs

2 teaspoons vanilla extract

2 cups (one 12-ounce package) chocolate chips

[handwritten: → Choose different choc chip - NOT Guirodelli]

Combine the flour, oatmeal, baking powder, baking soda, and salt in a medium bowl and set aside. In a large bowl, cream the butter and the sugars with an electric mixer until light and fluffy. Add the eggs one at a time, mixing well after each addition. Add the vanilla and mix it in well. Add the flour mixture and blend into the dough. Mix in the chocolate chips.

Form the dough into 2-tablespoon balls and place on a wax-paper-lined cookie sheet. Freeze for 30 minutes. Transfer the dough balls to an airtight container or freezer bag and freeze for up to 2 months.

When the urge strikes, take a couple of dough balls out of the freezer. Pop them in a preheated 375°F oven for 8 minutes. Reduce heat to 325°F and bake for an additional 8 minutes. Let the cookies rest in the baking pan for 5 minutes and eat them hot and melty, or transfer to a rack to cool.

Makes about 24 large cookies.

CENTS-ABLE SOLUTIONS: DOLLAR-STRETCHING DOT-COMS

The Web abounds with blogs, sites, and boards with tips and ideas for frugal living. You can spend a lot of time searching them, and you're sure to find your favorites. Some lean toward the crunchy "live off the land" side of frugal, while others scream with glee at two-for-one offers on Velveeta®. Below are some of the better sites I've found, with information that anyone can use.

www.stretcher.com

More than 350,000 penny pinchers visit Gary Forman's site to share ideas and support for people living frugal lifestyles — either by choice or because of circumstances. Experts in everything from personal finance to cooking inexpensive cuts of meat are frequent contributors. Free newsletters offer general tips and specific ideas for families.

www.frugalvillage.com

Sara Noel, author of the syndicated column "Frugal Living," has scores of eco-friendly, simple ideas for gracious living that is frugal, but never cheap. The information is well organized and easy to search, and there is an active forum where you can find help, support, and advice.

www.heloise.com

The doyenne of DIY's site has lots of hints and solutions for nearly every household dilemma. You can also sign up for a free daily hint sent via e-mail.

www.budgetsavvy.com

"Smart spending, rich living" is the tagline of this online magazine. There are dozens of detailed articles on all aspects of budget living, from gardening to tax tips. Founder Melissa Tosetti walks the talk — she documents her family's forays into gardening and shares travel and decorating tips that don't sacrifice style.

www.epicurious.com

Epicurious is the collected culinary wisdom of *Bon Appétit, Gourmet, Parade,* and *Self* magazines. It's the go-to source when you're looking for recipes for specific ingredients. The detailed and easy-to-use search form allows you to dig for recipes by cuisine, ingredient, course, dietary restrictions, and more.

www.greatdepressioncooking.com

In 2007, 92-year-old Clara Cannucciari's family wanted to preserve the memories and recipes she had shared with them over the years. The warmth and wit that helped Clara survive the Great Depression are evident in every word, and she graciously shares her simple tips for living a good life, including "Five Tips for Surviving Hard Times" and "Recipes for a Recession." The videos have become a YouTube sensation, and a cookbook and DVD are in the works.

www.consumerqueen.com

Melissa Garcia once walked out of the grocery store with $1,880 worth of food for which she paid a whopping $19. Her website doesn't promise you'll get that kind of savings (and she doesn't save that much every week, either) but she does offer a lot of resources for coupons, sales, reward programs, and cheap groceries.

www.fabandfru.com

Fabulous and Frugal gals Brandi Savitt and Stephanie Berenbaum bring readers advice from renowned financial and lifestyle experts as well as witty articles based on their own experiences in frugal living.

www.fallenfruit.org

Fallen Fruit is an art collaboration that

began with maps of public fruit: the fruit trees growing on or over public property in Los Angeles. Their projects have expanded to include Community Fruit Tree Plantings, Nocturnal Fruit Forages, and Public Fruit Jams, in which citizens bring homegrown or public fruit and join in communal jam making. From these projects they produce images, videos, and installations for a variety of public spaces.

The only real stumbling block is fear of failure. In cooking you've got to have a what-the-hell attitude.

— Julia Child

CHAPTER 9
THRIFTY GIFTS

Financial expert Suze Orman advises that one of the ways to have a good relationship with money is to give it away. Being generous is good for the soul, and thrifty does not mean stingy!

The lucky recipient of a homemade gift from you gets not only a wonderful present, but the priceless gift of your time, creativity, and personal touch.

Start collecting jars, baskets, and containers to use for wrapping homemade gifts. It's easy to remove the labels from most jars after they've had a 15-minute bath in a so-

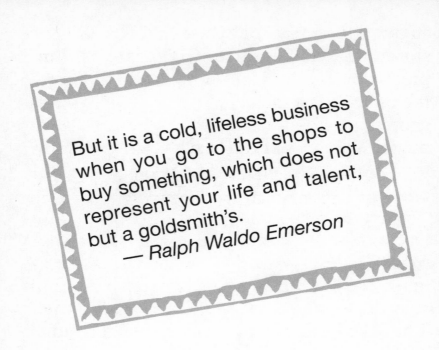

But it is a cold, lifeless business when you go to the shops to buy something, which does not represent your life and talent, but a goldsmith's.
— *Ralph Waldo Emerson*

lution of 1 part water and 1 part ammonia, and screen-printed labels can be removed with a craft knife.

TASTY TOKENS

A yummy gift from your kitchen is always welcome — you don't have to worry about getting the right size, color, or style — everyone likes to eat!

When I was a kid, my mom made cookie baskets at Christmas and Hanukkah for friends, family, co-workers, and teachers. For weeks the house smelled constantly of sugar and vanilla and the filled baskets were stored on every surface. One year she found pretty, perfectly sized baskets in Chinatown for only 25 cents each — she bought all the shop had, then made several trips to buy more. We had stacks of those baskets around for many years, and she still serves bread in one of them more than 30 years later.

When I was on my own, I followed her tradition of homemade cookies, with a slight twist. Instead of an assortment of cookies, I made each giftee a single gingerbread man-shaped cookie decorated to look like them. The likeness was not exact, but I'd add a baseball cap for a sports fan, thin ropes of dough hair for the lady with long locks, or a monogrammed T-shirt to personalize the cookies.

These edible gifts keep well at room temperature or in the freezer, so you can start early in the season and have plenty for everyone on your list.

Hot Chocolate on a Spoon

12 ounces chocolate, milk or semisweet, chopped OR 2 cups chocolate chips

20 heavy-duty plastic spoons

Melt the chocolate in the microwave or in a double boiler over low heat, stirring until

smooth. Dip a spoon in the chocolate,
moving it around to cover most of the
bowl of the spoon. Set the spoon down
on a sheet of waxed paper to cool.

Wrap the bowl of the spoon in plastic wrap,
and tie with a ribbon.

Spoons can be stirred into warm milk to
make hot chocolate or hot coffee for a
flavored café treat.

Makes 20 spoons.

Honey Lemon Teaspoons

1/2 cup honey

2 cups sugar

1 tablespoon white vin-
egar

1/4 cup water

peel of 1 lemon, cut into
strips (yellow part only,
no white pith)

20 heavy-duty plastic spoons

Place all of the ingredients in a large heavy-
bottomed saucepan and bring to a boil.
Brush the sides of the pan with a wet pastry brush when sugar crystals form. Boil
until the candy reaches the hard-crack
stage (when a drop of the molten candy in
a glass of cold water gets hard instantly)
— about 375°F on a candy thermometer
— 8 to 10 minutes. Remove from heat
and let the candy cool for 5 minutes.

Lay a sheet of aluminum foil on the counter, and place a wooden spoon in the
middle.

Dip a plastic spoon in the candy, moving it
around to fill most of the bowl with the
candy. Set the spoon down on the foil,
resting its handle on the handle of the
wooden spoon to keep the candy in the
bowl of the spoon. Let cool completely.

Wrap the bowl of the spoon in plastic wrap

or cellophane, and tie with a ribbon.

Spoons can be stirred into hot tea or even hot water to make a sweet, soothing treat.

DESSERTS WITH BENEFITS

These luscious fruit gifts have an extra benefit. The seeds, pits, and kernels can be used to make flavorful syrup. This trick was developed in the kitchen at Alice Waters's famed Chez Panisse, where perfect organic ingredients are used to the utmost of their ability to give.

Berry Sauce

4 pints fresh raspberries or blackberries

1 tablespoon lemon juice or orange juice

**FRUGAL FOODIE TIP:
THRIFTY FLATWARE**

Instead of using plastic spoons, scour thrift stores and yard sales for pretty silver teaspoons and demitasse spoons.

3/4 cup sugar

1/4 cup Simple Seed Syrup (recipe, page 286)

Place the berries in a fine sieve set over a bowl. Force the berries through the sieve with a wooden spoon, pressing and scraping to release as much liquid as possible. (Reserve seeds to make Simple Seed Syrup; recipe, page 286.)

Put the strained berry liquid, lemon juice, sugar, and Simple Seed Syrup in a medium saucepan, and stir to combine. Simmer over medium-low heat for 10 minutes. Ladle sauce into clean jars. Let stand until cool, then cover and store, refrigerated, for up to 2 weeks.

Makes about 4 cups.

Cherry Pie Filling

1/4 cup water

3/4 cup sugar

2 tablespoons lemon juice

2 teaspoons ground cinnamon

3 tablespoons cornstarch

2 pounds cherries, about 6 cups, pitted (pits reserved to make Simple Seed Syrup; recipe, page 286)

Combine water, sugar, lemon juice, and cinnamon in a large, heavy pot over medium-high heat, and slowly bring to a boil. Mix the cornstarch with 1 tablespoon of water and slowly drizzle into the syrup, stirring constantly. Add fruit and bring back to a boil, cooking for about 5 minutes, stirring constantly.

Ladle preserves into sterilized jars. Let stand until cool. Cover, and store, refrigerated, for up to 1 month, or for longer storage, see the section on canning on page 287.

To make a pie, bring the filling to room temperature. Pour into an unbaked 9-inch pie shell and dot with a tablespoon of cold butter cut into bits. Bake at 450°F for 30 minutes. Reduce heat to 350°F and bake for 30 minutes longer.

Apricot Preserves

2 1/2 pounds apricots (about 30)

5 apricot kernels (tip, page 286)

3 cups sugar

1/4 cup water

juice of one lemon

Cut the apricots in half, and remove the pits. Reserve pits to make Simple Seed

FRUGAL FOODIE TIP: PIN THE PIT

Use a large, heavy-duty bobby pin as a cherry pitter. Stick the looped end of the pin into the stem end of the cherry, past the pit, and then twist your wrist and flick it out.

To make a handle for your pitter, stick the pointy ends of the pin in a wine or Champagne cork.

Syrup (recipe follows).

Cut the apricots into 1-inch chunks. In a large, heavy-bottomed pot, combine the apricots, kernels, sugar, and water. Stir to combine.

Bring to a boil, stirring constantly. Cook, stirring frequently with a wooden spoon, until thickened, about 15 minutes. While the apricots are cooking, skim off the foam with a spoon. Save the foam in a small glass container; it settles into a tasty syrup. Remove the apricots from the heat and stir in the lemon juice.

Ladle preserves into sterilized jars. Let stand until cool. Cover and store, refrigerated, for up to 1 month, or for longer storage, see the section on canning on page 178.

Makes about 4 cups.

Simple Seed Syrup

seeds from 1 pint of raspberries or blackberries OR 10–12 apricot kernels OR 1 cup

**FRUGAL FOODIE TIP:
GETTING TO THE KERNEL**

Place the apricot pits on a dish towel. Cover with another dish towel, and smash them with a hammer, exposing the kernels inside. It's easiest to do on the floor, outside on the sidewalk, or on a very hard cutting board — marble works well, if you have one.

Apricot kernels impart an almondlike perfume to apricot preserves, and can also be dried and ground and used as a spice in recipes. The flavor is quite strong, so go easy and taste as you go.

of cherry pits

1 strip of lemon or orange peel, pith removed

3 cups water

1/2 cup sugar

Place seeds, pits, or kernels in a medium saucepan with peel and water, and bring to a boil. Boil until reduced to 1/2 cup of liquid, about 20–30 minutes. Strain the seeds, pits, or kernels from the water and discard; return the water to the pan. Add the sugar and bring to a boil. Reduce heat and simmer for 3–4 minutes. Remove from the heat and let the mixture cool completely.

Use this fruit-scented syrup to flavor iced tea, cocktails, lemonade, or raspberry sauce.

Makes 3/4 cup.

Put Up or Shut Up — Canning Made Easy

Sterilize canning jars by running them through a dishwasher with no detergent or simmering them in lots of water for 8–10 minutes. Place the lids in simmering water for 5 minutes to soften the rubber seals. Fill jars to within 3/4 inch of the rim with the hot fruit or jam. Wipe off the rim with a clean, warm, wet dishcloth, and seal the jar with the lid and metal ring. Place a cooling rack in the bottom of a large pot of boiling water. Place the jars in the water on the rack, not touching. Cover and boil for 20 minutes.

You don't need a fancy jar-lifter — just wrap thick rubber bands around the ends of a pair of tongs. Remove the jars with the prepped tongs and let them cool to room temperature. Check the seals after 24 hours. If properly sealed, the lids should be indented in the middle and should not

Once my jars were labeled, I felt contentedly thrilled with myself, as if I had pulled off a wonderful trick. People feel this way when they bake bread or have babies, and although they are perfectly entitled to feel that way, in fact, nature does most of the work.
— *Laurie Colwin*

respond to being pressed. If the seal seems fishy, just store that jar in the fridge and use within a month.

Not Your Bubbe's Biscotti

"Look at all of the fancy-schmancy mandel bread!"

That's what I imagine my great-grandmother Mimi would have said had she lived long enough to see the platters and jars of dipped and decorated biscotti at upscale coffee shops. I grew up eating her mandel bread, a twice-baked almond cookie very similar to biscotti.

Mimi's recipe contained butter and the result was a little more cookielike than these. My biscotti are not only less expensive, but very crisp and hold up very well to dunking in coffee, tea, or wine.

2 eggs

3/4 cup sugar

2 cups flour

1 teaspoon baking soda

3/4 cup almonds, toasted and coarsely chopped

Preheat oven to 350°F.

Line a baking sheet with foil and grease well.

Beat the eggs and sugar in the bowl of an electric mixer until pale, about 2 minutes. Beat in the flour and baking soda and continue beating until blended. Mix in the almonds. With floured hands, form half of the dough into a 12-inch log. Place on the baking sheet and press down to flatten to a width of about 3 inches. Repeat with the remaining dough.

Bake the cookie loaves for 30 minutes. Remove from the oven, leaving the oven on. Let the loaves cool for 5 minutes in the pan, then remove them to a cutting board. Slice each loaf diagonally into 12 slices with a sharp serrated knife. Don't press hard, let the knife do the work for you.

Put the slices back on the cookie sheet, laying them on their sides. Return them to the oven and bake for an additional 20 minutes. Cool completely on a rack.

Cookies will keep for about a week in an airtight container, or for up to 3 months in the freezer.

Makes 24 cookies.

Variations

COCOASCOTTI

Replace 1/4 cup of flour with cocoa powder.

CIOCCOLATO

Dip one side of the cooled cookies in melted white or dark chocolate. Place on waxed paper to cool and harden.

BAMBINIS

Divide the dough into 4 logs, each 8 inches long, and slice them to make cute little mini-cookies.

ZENZERO

Add 1 1/2 tablespoon chopped crystallized ginger with the eggs and sugar and 1 teaspoon ground cinnamon with the flour.

LIMONE E PAPAVERO

Add the grated zest of one lemon and three tablespoons of poppy seeds with the eggs and sugar.

The Frugal Beauty

The world makes endless attempts to separate women from their hard-earned cash in pursuit of youth and beauty, but most dermatologists will tell you that simple, homemade products are just as beneficial to your skin as the expensive "miracles in a jar." Your friends will gobble up these delicious treats that feed outer body and inner soul.

And while you're whipping up beauty treats for your pals, set aside some for yourself and have a "Vidal Sassoon" night. Like many of my great ideas, this cheap night of beauty

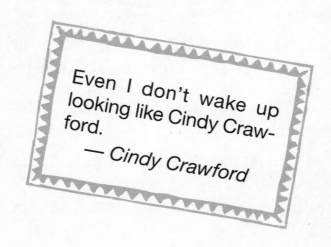

Even I don't wake up looking like Cindy Crawford.

— Cindy Crawford

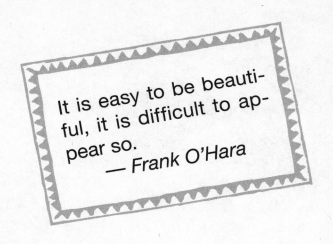

It is easy to be beautiful, it is difficult to appear so.
— Frank O'Hara

treatments was inspired by a childhood TV show. *The Facts of Life* was an 80s-era sitcom set in a snooty girl's boarding school. Most of the students came from wealthy families, but street-smart Jo Polniaczek was a wisecracking heroine to working-class girls. On one episode, she told her roomies that she and her waitress mom would have weekly "Vidal Sassoon" nights. They'd wash and set each other's hair, do mani-pedis, flip through a beauty magazine, and chitchat. She made it sound like more fun than an afternoon at a Beverly Hills spa.

Whether you have a Vidal Sassoon night with your mom, daughter, sister, friend, or on your own, it's an inexpensive indulgence that will leave you feeling like a queen!

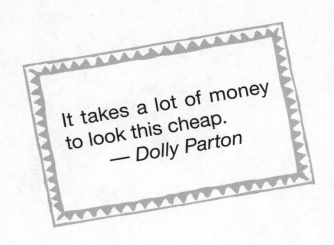

It takes a lot of money
to look this cheap.
— *Dolly Parton*

Fabulous Facial Truffles

12 bars of minisize hotel soap OR 3 bars of white unscented soap

1/4 cup oatmeal

2 tablespoons water

24 minimuffin cups

Grate the soap with a hand grater or in a food processor. Mix in the oatmeal and water to moisten. Microwave in a bowl for about 1 1/2 to 2 1/2 minutes, until the soap mixture expands and is bubbly. Add a little more water if it seems dry. Carefully remove the bowl from the microwave and stir. Spoon the mixture into well-oiled minimuffin cups and smooth the tops. Cool completely, then wrap in plastic wrap or cellophane and tie with ribbons.

Makes 24 soap truffles.

Sugar-Free Spa "Candy"

12 pieces of clean, natural-fiber fabric scraps, approximately 8 inches x 8 inches. Use muslin, vintage handkerchiefs, cheesecloth, washcloths, or linens.

1 1/2 cups oatmeal

1 1/2 cups dried mixed herbs (rosemary, mint, sage, thyme, bay, lavender)

3/4 cups grated soap

ribbon or string

Lay a piece of fabric on a flat surface. Place 2 tablespoons of oatmeal, 2 tablespoons of herbs, and 1 tablespoon of soap in the center. Roll the fabric around the ingredients and tie on each end with ribbons or string. Each piece of "candy" can be moistened in the shower or bath and used as a scrubber.

Makes 12 soap "candies."

Time for Tub Tea

1 1/2 cups powdered milk

1/2 cup Epsom salt

1/8 cup baking soda

2 tablespoons cornstarch

1/2 cup oatmeal

1/4 cup dried rosemary

1/4 cup chamomile tea

FOR WRAPPING

muslin or cheesecloth

12 lengths of ribbon, approximately 12 inches each

Mix the tea ingredients in a bowl. Spoon 1/4 cup of the bath tea into the center of an 8-inch square of muslin or double

FRUGAL BEAUTY TIP: SWAP TILL YOU DROP

Host a clothing swap! Gather a gaggle of gals and ask them to bring clean, good-quality clothing that no longer fits — or that they're just tired of looking at. Divide the clothes by type — sweaters here, skirts there — and let the ladies have at the piles. Each one gets a clean closet and a few free items, and any leftovers can be donated.

layer of cheesecloth — or, if you're feeling extra crafty, make a small drawstring bag. Gather the cloth into a bundle and tie tightly with ribbon. Tie another knot at about 1 inch from the top of the ribbon, making a long loop that can be hung over the faucet of the bath, so the hot water will fall over the bag and brew the tea as the tub fills.

Makes 12 tea bags.

That's the Way the Bath Cookie Crumbles

1 1/2 cups Epsom salt

1/2 cup oatmeal

1/2 cup baking soda

1/2 cup cornstarch

2 teaspoons ground cinnamon

2 tablespoons olive oil

1 teaspoon vitamin E oil, baby oil, or your favorite massage oil

2 eggs

Preheat oven to 350°F.

Mix all ingredients in a large bowl. Gently roll dough into 1-inch balls. Place dough balls on an ungreased cookie sheet. Bake bath cookies for 10 minutes, until lightly browned. Remove from the oven and allow to cool completely.

Crumble 2 cookies into a warm bath.

Makes 24 bath cookies.

Pump Up the Shower Jam

2 cups water

2 envelopes unflavored gelatin

3 cups unscented liquid hand soap

food coloring

Bring water to a boil in a large saucepan. Remove from heat and slowly add gelatin, stirring until it is dissolved. Slowly add liquid soap and stir to mix. Pour liquid into a clean clear jar or container, and chill overnight. Add one or two drops of food coloring. (More might stain the

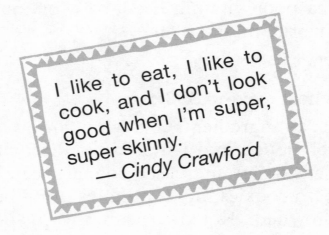

I like to eat, I like to cook, and I don't look good when I'm super, super skinny.
— Cindy Crawford

bath or shower.)

Spoon into small, pretty jars — old spice jars work great. Store in the fridge for up to 3 weeks. Use as you would shower gel,

FRUGAL BEAUTY TIP: SAY "POO-POO" TO SHAMPOO

Recent studies have shown that shampooing your hair every day actually makes your hair oilier and less manageable. You can prevent damage to your hair and wallet by replacing 2–3 shampoos a week with a baking soda rinse. Put 1–2 tablespoons of baking soda in the bottom of a 16-ounce water bottle. Fill the bottle with warm water. Starting at one side of the hairline, squirt the baking soda solution in sections and finger it through your hair. Follow up with a cider vinegar conditioning rinse once a week. Put 1–2 tablespoons of cider vinegar in the same bottle, fill with warm water, and do the same hairline routine. Dry and style as usual.

with a sponge, loofah, or mesh scrubber. *Makes 6 1/2-cup "servings."*

Wake Up and Smell the Coffee Scrub

3 cups packed brown sugar

3 cups granulated sugar

1 cup ground coffee

1 cup oil — almond, olive, baby oil, or massage oil

1/4 cup honey

1 tablespoon vanilla extract

Mix all ingredients. Spoon into small, pretty jars — old spice jars work great. Store in the fridge for up to 3 weeks. To use, scoop out about a tablespoon of the

You give but little when you give of your possessions. It is when you give of yourself that you truly give.

— *Kahlil Gibran*

WORTH ITS SALT

A soak in an Epsom-salt bath is not only luxurious, but can also improve your health! The main ingredient in Epsom salt is magnesium — which most of us don't get enough of in our diet. Soaking in Epsom salt can offer many of the same heath benefits of magnesium in food, such as:

- Reducing inflammation
- Improving heart and circulatory health
- Flushing toxins and heavy metals from the cells, relieving muscle pain and aching joints and helping the body to eliminate harmful substances
- Improving the body's ability to use insulin
- Improving nerve function by regulating electrolytes, and helping to maintain proper calcium levels in the blood
- Reducing stress. Magnesium is necessary for the body to bind adequate amounts of serotonin, a mood-elevating chemical within the brain that creates a feeling of well-being and relaxation.

scrub and slather it on your arms, neck, and shoulders. Rinse, then wash with your regular shower cleanser.

Seasoned Bath Salt

3 cups Epsom salt

1 teaspoon glycerin*

1 1/2 cups baking soda

3 tablespoons ground cinnamon

Mix all ingredients. Spoon into small, pretty jars — old spice jars work great. Store in the fridge up to 3 weeks.

Makes 6 1/2-cup "servings."

*Glycerin is a colorless, odorless liquid commonly added to soaps and other toiletries for smoothness and moisture. It can be found in the skin care section of most drugstores.

CENTS-ABLE SOLUTIONS: RESTAURANT RECESSIONISTA

My son once had an assignment to interview a family member, and he asked my mom what was different for her as a kid than for him. The first thing she said was "We almost never went to restaurants. It was a real treat when we did."

When you're eating frugally and doing most of your own cooking, a night out is indeed a treat — and one you don't have to feel guilty about indulging. You can relax while someone else figures out how to stretch the ingredients and does the dishes.

With just a few smart decisions and tweaks to your dining out routine, you can enjoy a waiter-delivered meal without starving your bank account.

- Go for lunch instead of dinner. Your favorite spots have the same great food at lunch, usually at a lower price.

- Stretch your plate. Portions are no-toriously huge at many restaurants. You can almost always stretch your dining dollar to cover at least two meals. As soon as your food comes to the table, cut the portions in half with your fork. Slide half the food to the side of your plate and don't touch it until you've finished the first half. You'll probably find that you're satisfied after eating half the meal. If you think you'll be tempted to clean your plate, you can ask your waiter for a doggy bag at the beginning of the meal.

- Skip the extras: appetizers, desserts, wine, and cocktails. You'll still have the pleasure of a night out, and cut 25–50 percent off your bill.

- Avoid chain restaurants. The quality of the food is not worth your time and money. Even in the smallest town you can find a mom and pop Chinese restaurant, taqueria, or deli serving up soulful, chef-made fare.

- If you're on the road or in a real tourist trap, chain restaurants may be your only option. If so, scour the Internet for coupons for free kids' meals, appetizers, and other discounts.
- Buy a local Entertainment Book. They're deeply discounted a few months into the calendar year, and can save you a lot of money at local places. If you're traveling and will be in a city for a week or more, buy a book for that city as well. Visit www.entertainment.com for prices, locations, and details.
- BYOW. Even with a corkage fee, you'll spend less than even the least expensive bottle.
- Head to Happy Hour! Lots of great restaurants, especially those in business districts, offer filling snacks at deep discounts between 4:00 and 6:00 P.M. It's a great way to eat for less, especially before an early movie or theater showtime.
- You *can* take it with you. Order your food to go and you'll be less

tempted to add additional dishes. Have your honey set the table with crystal and candles while you run out to pick up the chow.

- If your young kids don't eat much, don't bother to order them a meal. Some of the food from your plate will probably be more than enough.
- Restaurants.com has discounted gift certificates for local, nonchain restaurants. Typical deals include $10 gift certificates for $3 and $25 gift certificates for $10. There are often restrictions, such as minimum food purchases, guaranteed gratuities, and blackout days, but you can save serious dough and may find a new favorite spot.
- Don't skimp on the tip! Good service always deserves a tip of at least 20 percent.

ACKNOWLEDGMENTS

Muchas grácias to Brenda Knight, Felice Newman, and the team at Viva Editions — your support and enthusiasm mean the world. *Xie xie* to Mark Rhynsburger, Scott Idleman, and Frank Wiedemann for making me look so much better than I am. *Danke schön* to Tom Super and the American Meat Institute; Brandi Savitt, Stephanie Berenbaum, and Karie Reynolds of Fabulous & Frugal; Peter Smolowitz and the Epsom Salt Council; Peter Shankman and the other generous HARO contributors — you're what the Internet is all about. *Merci* buckets to friends and family who graciously contributed ideas, tips, and memories: Beth Enard, Susan Eslick, Danielle Fogel, Maria Hjelm, Kirsten Mellor, Ted Michon, Meredith Morris, Audryn Lovinger, Kathy Osler, Daphne Philips, Joel Patrick Rose, and Ruthy Weil. *Domo arigato* to my Facebook friends — your notes, comments, updates, and support make long, lonely days of writing much less long and lonely. And *mille, mille grazie* to John and Max Starr, who make every day delicious.

Without one cook giving another cook a tip or two, human life might have died out a long time ago.
— *Laurie Colwin*

Let's have delicious fun saving dough to-gether!

Please keep in touch — I'd love to know your
favorite frugal foods, and I'm sharing more
of mine on my blog.

Frugal_Foodie@yahoo.com
http://frugalfoodiecookbook.blogspot.com

ABOUT THE AUTHORS

The coauthor of *The Party Girl Cookbook,* **LARA STARR** has offered advice on easy, affordable cooking and entertaining on TV, radio, newspapers, magazines, and websites throughout the US and Canada. She lives in Marin County, CA. Read about her culinary adventures at cakestarr.blogspot.com.

LYNETTE SHIRK is a classically trained chef, and has authored nine cookbooks. She has cooked at Chez Panisse, Wolfgang Puck's Postrio, Bizou, and other celebrated restaurants. The author of *The Mother Daughter Cookbook* and *Wild Women in the Kitchen,* she lives in Seattle, WA.